LIVING THE SINGAPORE STORY

*We dedicate this book to the memory of
our founding Prime Minister, Lee Kuan Yew*

Published by National Library Board, Singapore

National Library Board, Singapore
100 Victoria Street
#14-01 National Library Building
Singapore 188064
Tel: +65 6332 3255
email: ref@library.nlb.gov.sg
www.nlb.gov.sg
All rights reserved.

Printed by KHL Printing Co. Pte Ltd

National Library Board, Singapore Cataloguing-in-Publication Data

Cheong, Suk Wai

Living the Singapore story : celebrating our 50 years, 1965-2015 / writers,
Cheong Suk Wai, Jennani Durai, Cassandra Chew; editor, Angelina Choy;
supervising editor, Han Fook Kwang. – Singapore : National Library Board,
[2015]
pages cm.

ISBN 978-981-4342-98-8 (Hardback)
ISBN 978-981-4342-99-5 (Paperback)

1. Singaporeans – Anecdotes. 2. National characteristics, Singaporean.
3. Resilience (Personality trait). 4. Singapore – Anecdotes. I. Jennani Durai,
author. II. Chew, Cassandra, author. III. Choy, Angelina, editor.
IV. Han, Fook Kwang, editor. V. Title.

DS609
959.5705 — dc23   OCN 905587254

LIVING
THE
SINGAPORE
STORY

Celebrating our 50 years
1965 – 2015

Contents

About this Book

What is the Singapore Story? A newly independent, multiracial country without any natural resources struggling to find its place in the sun. The story of how a Third World country made the transformation to become the modern, thriving metropolis it is today.

It is all these and more. But most of all, it is a story of its people, mostly poor in the beginning, who were determined to overcome the odds together so that they could provide a better future for their children.

This is a book of their stories – ordinary Singaporeans and some better-known ones – who, through the lives they led, the work they did and the interests they pursued, collectively make the Singapore Story.

They come from all walks of life: hawker, bus conductor, nurse, scientist, teacher, army officer, doctor, architect, athlete, playwright, and reflect the diversity of the nation – Chinese, Malays, Indians, Eurasians, young and old. But every one of them with a Singapore story to tell.

As the nation celebrates its 50th birthday, this book – commissioned by the National Library Board and produced by Straits Times Press – is our tribute to the people of Singapore.

Revellers snapping photos of President Tony Tan Keng Yam during the National Day Parade held at the Marina Bay Floating Platform on 9 August 2013.

Photo by DESMOND LUI

President's Message

We celebrate the 50th anniversary of Singapore's independence this year. Fifty years is a relatively short span in the context of nations. But in this short time, we have made remarkable progress in all aspects, whether it is our physical infrastructure, economy, social well-being or national security. Our achievements can be attributed to a combination of various factors: honest and visionary leaders, a capable public service and a resilient people who pulled together.

I am glad that this book focuses on the people of Singapore. The story of Singapore is made up of the personal stories of Singaporeans from all walks of life and across cultures and religions. The Singapore that we love is established on the hard work and sacrifice of individuals.

This book highlights the can-do spirit, courage and determination of our people as the special ingredients that enabled Singapore to transform from a Third World country to become the thriving metropolis and vibrant society that we are today. I am confident that if we continue to work together as one united people, Singapore will continue to progress and become a stronger nation and a better home for all Singaporeans in the years to come.

Dr Tony Tan Keng Yam
President of the Republic of Singapore

Prime Minister Lee Hsien Loong in a photograph with Singaporean students during a reception for Singaporeans living in Brisbane. The photo was taken at Tattersall's Club on 16 November 2014 after the end of the G20 leaders' summit, which PM Lee attended.

Photo by SEAH KWANG PENG

Foreword

The success or failure of a country depends, to a large extent, on the quality of its leaders and people.

This book is about the people of Singapore. It tells the story of Singapore through the personal stories of 58 of us. These 58 Singaporeans are a microcosm of Singapore.

These are stories of grit. After Singapore was cast out of the Federation of Malaysia, our prospects were bleak. The future was uncertain. But the people of Singapore never lost hope. They responded to the clarion call of our first Prime Minister, Lee Kuan Yew, to join him in building a metropolis and a nation. They overcame individual difficulties with grit and determination, and succeeded.

These are stories of resilience. Hundreds of thousands of our people were relocated from *kampungs* and squatter settlements into high-rise HDB flats. Many had to give up traditional ways of earning a living to learn new skills and work in factories. Singaporeans took these massive changes in their stride, seized the new opportunities and thrived.

These are stories of unity in diversity. They tell of people of different races and religions, different backgrounds, living and working together, pursuing their passions and playing different roles, building this nation together.

These stories tell how far we have come in the last 50 years. They remind us of the values that got us here. They inspire us to write our own stories with the same grit, resilience and unity. Fifty years from now, may our children and grandchildren be able to rejoice and take pride in what we have built, and tell as good a story of Singapore through the lives of our generation.

Lee Hsien Loong
Prime Minister
Republic of Singapore

Children enjoying a free performance of Chinese street opera, or *wayang*, at George Street in this photo taken in October 1975.

Photo by FRANCIS ONG

Jobs of a different nature were evident in the earlier years.

(top left) Farmer Neo Siak San washes his pigs at Seletar East Farmway 2 in this photo taken in 1987. Pig breeding was phased out in the 1980s due to health and environmental concerns. Photo by LESLEY KOH

(above) PC 1159, or Abdul Haji Mohamed, 45, was a fixture at the junction of Kim Seng and River Valley roads, directing traffic at one of the busiest intersections. The traffic cop's expert handling earned him three commendations in the five years he was on duty there until he retired in 1972. Photo by JERRY SEH

(left) Workers on the job at Ford Motor Factory in Bukit Timah in this photo taken in March 1966. The factory, which opened in 1941 as Ford's first assembly plant in Southeast Asia, was where the British surrendered to the Japanese in 1942. It resumed operations after the war and closed in June 1980. Photo from SINGAPORE PRESS HOLDINGS

(right) These boys selling *ma pew poh* on the roadside dice with death every weekend as they run in between vehicles selling Chinese newspapers with the day's horse racing results. This photo was taken in July 1971. Photo by WAN SENG YIP

(left) Reflecting the spirit of Chinese New Year are these happy girls strolling at the Botanic Gardens. This photo was taken in 1969, on the first day of the Year of the Rooster.
Photo by CHRISTOPHER LOH

(top) Muslim families at Kampong Ubi preparing for Hari Raya were undeterred by the October 1973 floods. As soon as waters began to rise, this family, their spirits still high, moved the earthern cookers onto tables and resumed their cooking in knee-high water.
Photo by JUNID JUANI

(left) Students checking their examination results as a teacher writes them on a blackboard at River Valley English School in November 1967.
Photo by WAN SENG YIP

(bottom left) Children letting off firecrackers during Chinese New Year in January 1971. Firecrackers were banned in 1972 for safety reasons.
Photo by MAK KIAN SENG

(bottom right) In the true spirit of *gotong royong*, or community help, Kampong Ubi residents help to repair a road off Jalan Ubi. Even the children, as seen in this July 1973 photo, came out to lend a hand. Photo by JUNID JUANI

(left and bottom left) The Istana opens its grounds on some public holidays. These children were there in September 1978 on Hari Raya Puasa. Other open days: Chinese New Year (below left, in a February 1975 photo), Deepavali, Labour Day and National Day. Top photo by YOW YUN WOH; Bottom photo by JUNID JUANI

(bottom right) Families in their holiday best turn the island resort of Sentosa into a playground on the Deepavali holiday in November 1975. Photo by MAHFUTZ MATTAR

19

(far left) Miss Tourism Singapura, Mollie Ang Mooi Hua, waving to the crowd along the Esplanade as she and other beauty queens sail along in their gaily decorated boats as part of the big Tourist Week Regatta in November 1966. Photo by KOK AH CHONG

(left) Marine Parade residents of all races throng staircase landings, corridors and even balcony ledges to get a glimpse of the Chingay procession passing by. The parade, at the junction of Marine Terrace and Marine Crescent, was held on 8 February 1978. Photo by YOW YUN WOH

Thousands taking part in Singapore's first National Day Parade that started in front of City Hall on 9 August 1966. The contingents, which included representatives from the army, navy, police, youth groups, cultural societies and schools, proceeded to march from the Padang to Tanjong Pagar Road.

Photo from SINGAPORE PRESS HOLDINGS

A NATION IS BORN

On 9 August 1965, Prime Minister Lee Kuan Yew announces Singapore's separation from Malaysia. It comes as a shock, but Mr Lee assures the people that everyone will have a place in the new nation of Singapore.

Photo by ALI YUSOFF

25

Happy to leave
the *kampung* behind

Unlike some, retired teacher Paul Fernandez, 75, was eager to live in
an apartment. He paid $12,500 for a flat in Queenstown, Singapore's first
public housing estate, in 1973 – and has lived there since

The government did not force us to leave the *kampungs*, but people with an axe to grind will tell you they did – they'll say the government set fires to *kampungs* and the fires pointed like an arrow to the HDB blocks where the government wanted them to live! But not me, I was happy to move. It was the trend, the modern way of life. So when the opportunity arose, I decided to "urbanise" myself.

My *kampung* was in Upper Bukit Timah, near Dairy Farm. It was quite inconvenient to keep living there. Early in the morning, the nightsoil workers would come, and the smell made me want to escape. There was also a lot of trouble from pests – insects and rodents.

I got married at the age of 20, while studying at the Teachers' Training College, and lived in the *kampung* with my wife until my first son was born. Many people used to stay in a house for a year or two, then move out, and other people would take over. That's how we, too, were always moving from place to place. So moving into this flat helped me feel settled for the first time.

When the first SIT (Singapore Improvement Trust) blocks came up around here, I visited some friends living there, and that made me want to live in an apartment block as well.

I didn't think I would get a flat in Queenstown, so I applied for a Farrer Road block. Then one day I got a call from the HDB: "There's a vacant flat in Queenstown. Do you want to buy this one instead of waiting?" So I said: "Of course." The flat had structural defects and other people had rejected it, but I took it eagerly, come what may! I found the defects the very first day – cracks in some walls. But the flat has held up for more than 40 years now.

Some residents, in the early days, started calling our block the "Butterfly Block" and the name stuck. It's called that because of the shape of the building – like a butterfly with its wings stretched out.

When we moved in, there were not many other blocks around. There was an open field on one side, and a jungle on the other – lots of trees. There was also an ABC brewery facing Alexandra Road. Over the years, more HDB blocks started coming up.

But it's true what they say about the *kampung* spirit. That did exist among the different races of people living in a *kampung*, and it's one of the few things I missed when I moved my family to an HDB flat.

You can bump into people in the lift or a coffeeshop and ask: "Where do you live?", only to find they are your next-door neighbour, and both of you never knew. There's a lot less interaction.

After I came here to settle down, I have never wanted to move, because of my past memories of having to move so much. There are some people now who sell their flat to make a profit, then spend that money, and buy another flat and do it all over again. But not me – the first time I urbanised myself, I stayed put.

Paul Fernandez was able to get his flat quickly because it had structural defects and some other people had rejected it. Despite the cracks in the walls, the flat has held up for more than 40 years now.

Liu Thai Ker trained under renowned architect IM Pei in New York. He returned to serve Singapore from 1969, and was chief executive of the HDB from 1979 till 1989, when he was appointed Singapore's chief planner till 1992.

I wanted HDB to be as good a brand as Chanel

Architect Liu Thai Ker, 77, joined the Housing Board in 1969,
and made public housing one of Singapore's finest achievements

One day in the early 1970s, my HDB colleague and I walked up a hill in Bukit Merah to see how squatters were coping with leaks in their slum. We were on a dirt road with no drains and it had just rained. Soon, water and human faeces came rolling down the hill towards us. I hadn't expected such a dramatic welcome!

Another time, I asked my colleagues where the worst slums in Singapore were. They took me to Smith Street in Chinatown – each family had a 3m by 3m space, separated from others by only a curtain, and they shared a toilet and kitchen. There was no sense of privacy, but they had a great sense of humour, which was a saving grace.

In the 27 years that the British ruled Singapore, they built only 32,000 public flats. They said they built so few because the construction industry here could not cope with more. But in 1960, our government said: "We're not going to use that as an excuse. We have to solve the housing problem." At that time, about 1.3 million among Singapore's 1.9 million-strong population were squatters. So the HDB hired anyone who wanted to be a contractor to build the many flats needed.

We built 189,299 HDB flats between 1960 and 1985, and by 1985, 80 per cent of Singaporeans lived in these flats.

After I joined the HDB, I asked psychologists how we could avoid people feeling depressed amid such high density? They said: "Make sure they can always see the sky." So that's what we did.

We stuck to a low budget because that was the only way we could spread the benefit to as many people as possible. We didn't put in any frills because we put all our money into creating the largest possible floor area for residents. That's because you can change just about anything in your flat except its floor area.

But while I put good housing before good architecture, my father Liu Kang was a famous painter and so I cared about aesthetics, too. Now, what's an aesthetic measure that costs nothing? Well, what's the difference between Miss Universe and an ordinary-looking girl? Proportion. So I spent a lot of time working out the proportions of windows, façades, and how the blocks lined up along a street.

In the 1970s and 1980s, people were ashamed to live in HDB flats because there was a stigma about living in such flats then, what with resettlement and all. So in 1985, when the HDB did not have to catch up with housing demand anymore, I asked my colleagues: "Why don't we bring private housing into HDB new towns?"

My estate officers supported that. When we called the first tender for this, I was nervous as hell. "Which private developer would want to come in?" I thought. But the response was overwhelmingly good, because HDB towns had all the facilities. I had designed these towns to be self-sufficient, to cut down on traffic heading downtown.

In those days, my HDB colleagues themselves would never admit they worked in the HDB because at that time, the quality of construction was quite poor and some designs were not carefully thought through. But I told them we had to change the image of the HDB such that every time people heard "HDB", they would think it was as good as the luxury fashion brand Chanel. My colleagues said: "You must be mad."

But I looked into every damn thing for quality control, from the quality of the tiles to workmanship. This was meaningful work. At my school, Chung Cheng High, I had been taught *da wo, xiao wo* (big me, little me); one worked for *da wo*, or put nation above self.

First First Lady: I wanted to do more than smile

Photo by NEO XIAOBIN

Noor Aishah Md Salim, 82, wife of the late Yusof Ishak – Singapore's first President – could not speak a word of English when, at age 26, she became First Lady. But determination changed that

One day in 1959, my husband Yusof Ishak came home and said: "I've resigned." He was the founder and editor-in-chief of the *Utusan Melayu* newspaper but that year, the Umno party had become the paper's big shareholder and tried to undermine my husband's authority. My husband told me: "Don't worry, God will give us *rezeki* (sustenance)." I didn't mind, even though we had three young children.

Shortly after Yusof quit, Lee Kuan Yew told him: "When we win the elections this year, I want you to be Singapore's first head of state." And my husband said: "There are many other people to choose from, and it's not like I know how to be a head of state." Mr Lee said: "We don't want anyone else."

On entering the Istana, I learnt everything I could and tried not to trouble anyone. My duties included raising funds for at least 14 charities and associations here. I also helped them get housing and other needs from the government. In entertaining guests at the Istana, my seven helpers and I prepared the food, as there was no hotel catering then. I didn't mind. Before we entered the Istana, I sewed my own *kebayas* and took apart Yusof's old shirts, studying the pieces to sew shirts for him. Friends asked: "How will you carry on like this?" I said: "Carry on, lah!"

At first, I would just smile whenever I met dignitaries and their wives as I couldn't speak English. I decided this would not do and got a Mrs Paley from a convent here to teach me. By 1967, just two years after Yusof became Singapore's first President, I could speak and write English. Then, in 1971, the University of Singapore conferred on me an honorary Doctor of Letters.

Among our most memorable visitors were Emperor Akihito and Empress Michiko of Japan. The Empress was so slim! I've always been rather round, and fretted so much about it that I went on a diet. But Yusof never minded about my weight; in fact, he urged me to enjoy my food.

Yusof died on 23 November 1970, aged 60. Mr Lee said the government would give me a pension of about $2,000 monthly, and that my three children and I could stay on in the Istana grounds as long as we liked. He knew we hadn't a house in Singapore. I said: "Thank you, but I will leave this house after 40 days." I felt it was not right to stay on. Mr Lee then enabled me to rent government quarters in Goodwood Hill, until I had a house built in Chestnut Crescent, on a plot Yusof had bought for his retirement.

Being a widow was hard at first; my mother and my eldest daughter Orkid were with me, but I still cried my eyes out. My son Imran, nicknamed Baba, was always studying, and my younger daughter Zuriana, whom I nicknamed Nyonya, was studying in London.

Yusof was 39, and I, 16, when my parents arranged for us to marry. I knew nothing about this until my father started saying: "There is this very good, intelligent bachelor who is older than you and who will take good care of you. If you marry a young man, your life would be uncertain." We had our *akad nikah* (marriage contract) ceremony on 20 November 1949 at the Sunshine Hotel in Penang. My family was there but Yusof hadn't told his family we would wed. My mother-in-law heard about us only when we were already in Singapore, and rushed down from Taiping to meet me. She said: "Oh, I'm happy he married you" and started teaching me how to cook her son's favourite dishes.

The streets of Singapore were quieter than Penang's, as well as dirtier and full of rickshaws. The house Yusof built had no lights or water; the authorities sent barrels of water to us daily, and at night, he would pump kerosene lamps. After a year, we had electricity and piped water, in time for Imran's birth.

By 1980, my children had settled down and, not being one to sit still, I began seeing the world with my many good friends. I've been to China twice, climbing mountains and cruising down the Yangtze, and South Korea and most of Europe.

It's good that Singapore honoured my husband as a pioneer. He was with me for only 21 years. Once, he said: "I think you and our children will have to face the world without me for a long time." I said: "Don't worry, I will bring them up well and keep your good name." God took Yusof away from me when he was only 60, but from our marriage I now have three children, 10 grandchildren and 12 great-grandchildren.

Noor Aishah Md Salim and her husband President Yusof pose in the bedroom of their house within the Istana grounds for a picture set up by the President with a tripod and a timer. The photo was taken in 1963.

Photo from NOOR AISHAH MD SALIM

Winston Choo became Singapore's first three-star general in 1988, at age 47. He is also Singapore's longest-serving Chief of Defence Forces, from 1974 to 1992.

Photo by KOK YUFENG

Beer in the army?
Thank Mr Lee Kuan Yew

Former defence chief Winston Choo, 74, recounts those rough-and-ready times of building a defence force from scratch and how second-hand tanks were a big morale-booster

Barely a year into my job as aide-de-camp to President Yusof Ishak, independent Singapore's first head of state, Deputy Prime Minister Goh Keng Swee, recalled me to the army. I'd trained as a professional soldier and Dr Goh told me that I was to train for the post of Chief Signals Officer and that, after various other appointments, I would be Chief of Defence Forces.

Singapore's security position then was very precarious. There were still many Malaysian soldiers stationed here, including a battalion at Temasek Camp in Ulu Pandan, home to Singapore's Second Infantry Regiment (2SIR). When 2SIR returned from a mission in Johor, it had to camp in tents in Farrer Park because the Malaysians would not move out. There were only 600 Singaporean soldiers here then, and as not everyone in the Malaysian Cabinet had agreed to separation, Malaysia could have taken Singapore back by force.

So the government had to form the defence forces here fast, and asked Britain, India and Egypt for help. Britain – I suspect it didn't want to offend Malaysia – devised a plan to form our forces that would have taken us 100 years to accomplish. India congratulated us. Egypt did not reply. Then we approached the Israelis who, crucially, agreed to advise, not command us. They would hold our hand in the initial stages, beginning with setting up a school to train our military leaders, and a ministry to drive all other developments.

Still, the Israelis wanted us to do everything the way they did, including banning alcohol in camp. So when Premier Lee Kuan Yew visited us and asked for a glass of beer, we said: "There is none." And he said: "What kind of army are we?" That's how we got our beer back.

Israeli privates can call generals by their first name. If our soldiers did that, our discipline would collapse. We adapt, not adopt.

We had to equip our forces quickly and so we took whatever Britain left behind after it withdrew its troops from Singapore in 1971, and bought everything else second-hand. These included 72 tanks from Israel, which we could parade on National Day. At that time, Malaysia did not have a single tank so when all these tanks rolled past Malaysian Premier Abdul Razak Hussein at the parade, that was the clincher! They had a tremendous effect on everyone.

When you are building an armed force, you take what you can. The most important thing is not the equipment, but the people who operate them – and force multipliers, by which I mean knowing what to do with the weapon you have, to meet your mission.

Later, we began to make self-loading rifles and machine guns and then developed our own technologies. Today, what differentiates Singapore's defence forces from others in the region is their ability to operate high-tech weapons. But in the end, what matters most is still boots on the ground because the days of robots fighting wars are still far away.

In 1974, at the age of 33, I became the fourth Director of General Staff of Singapore's armed forces, or what is now known as Chief of Defence Forces.

Up till then, everyone in the defence forces wore the same uniform – green. But I said: "I can't imagine a sailor in green, or the head of the navy being called General." So we had different uniforms and different commanders for each service. We sent our officers to various countries to train and then had them mingle with one another to exchange ideas.

I decided that, as we are so small, our strength comes from operating all our systems in harmony. So I formed a Joint Staff, in which anything on hard land is the army's responsibility, anything an inch above land is the airforce's watch and anything beyond an inch of water is the navy's. Getting everyone to work together was my biggest challenge because I was dealing with very strong personalities. The most effective way to lead is to have an open door policy. Many people came to see me with their concerns.

Once, I was at a hawker centre when a man came up to me. He said he had been a sergeant under me. He added: "Sir, you were a b*****d. But you were also very fair and I would follow you to war."

Those days, fists did the talking

Soldiers must be aggressive, says Siah Nah Nam, 68, who helped train the first army recruits in 1967. He should know – he was taught by the Israelis

When the first batch of NS recruits enlisted in 1967, I was among their trainers, but I was only two years older than they were. It was hard to discipline them – most of them were like gangsters and always wanted to challenge us and fight. If we were weak, they would bully us. So we had to resort to being physical to control them.

We would go behind the buildings, and I would take off my top because my corporal rank was on the shirt, and we'd slug it out. I would usually win because I was quite a fighter. In primary and secondary school I was caned publicly for fighting because I was very hot-tempered and violent.

We would tell the recruits: "Outside camp, you are the gangsters. We respect you. But in camp, we are the gangsters. And you must respect us." It did happen that an instructor was beaten up in Geylang by gangsters. When the camp commander heard, he sent several people to exact revenge. Then the CID (Criminal Investigation Department) sent officers to our camp, but the commander got wind of it and asked the men to hide. He protected his men and earned our respect.

Soldiers must be aggressive. We learnt to be tough under the Israelis who trained us. When we were doing drills and struggling to carry casualties on a stretcher from Lim Chu Kang to Safti, four to a stretcher and rotating among six men, the trainers scoffed at us. They said that in Israel, it would be just one man carrying a casualty, and in the desert.

They pushed us hard. So whatever we took from our trainers, we gave to the recruits. Training was really tough then. In one exercise, recruits had to frog-jump down four storeys of a building and do chin-ups before they could eat. And after lunch, they'd have to frog-jump back up. Many vomited.

A few recruits from rich families were brought down to earth. Some would cry when they had to cut grass or clean the toilets, as all their lives they had been served by others. Those who overslept were told to go back to camp on Sunday morning for "compulsory sleep". They had to lie down on the bed for one hour without fidgeting. After that punishment, they always woke up on time.

Because I was a bad student in school, my highest standard passed was Secondary 2. I left Gan Eng Seng School in 1964 without a certificate. But I was determined to become an officer, and studied for my O levels under the SAF Education Programme. I finally got my certificate in 1977 and joined the Officer Cadet School in 1979. I was 32 years old, the oldest recruit there. Even so, I wanted to get the Sword of Honour, but I was competing against 19-year-olds. So I had to be content with being in the top 10 per cent of more than 400 recruits – and I still got a sword.

While in the army, I also joined the Singapore Unarmed Training Institute, and graduated with a black belt in *khong chang* in 1972. Three years of martial arts training mellowed me, and I learnt to be more patient. I also realised how powerful my fists were. When my three kids were growing up – I wed in 1968 and the children came in 1968, 1970 and 1972 – I was careful to use only my finger tips to discipline them, and not my whole hand.

If you look at my wall where I hang my military plaques, best trainee awards and my sword, and ask me what my greatest achievement is, I'll say it is my children. I know how important having a family is, because my parents left me in the care of my uncle and aunt when they returned to China for political reasons when I was three. Two of my brothers left with them, and another was given away.

My aunt treated me badly, and that's why I wanted to get away from home. I applied in 1965 to join the volunteer force, then known as the Territorial Army. I was accepted in 1966 when I was 19 and could stay in the army barracks and get away from her nagging!

Spending 26 years in the army taught me a lot. The principles I live by, I learnt in the army. If you want to collect the pay, get the job done. Whatever task is given, do and do on time. Never give up.

That last principle really hit home when I was doing my airborne training. We had to complete two night jumps, one equipment jump and 10 main jumps. On my sixth jump, I hurt my leg. I hobbled through my next three jumps, but just couldn't make the 10th. I was given six months to finish the last jump, and I willed myself to do it. I finally got my wings. So you see, never give up.

(Clockwise, from top left) Siah Nah Nam (front) and fellow recruits resting during a long route march and doing the monkey crawl during his Section Leaders' Course at Safti. He graduated in 1967, and is seen in front of a three-tonner and sparring with a friend during his School of Signals days, and with fellow sergeants in front of a 106mm recoilless gun during 3SIR training.

Photos from SIAH NAH NAM

Tan Suan Yong had to deal with all kinds of obstacles in clearing land for Jurong industrial estate, including unexploded bombs, human remains and a burly squatter sharpening his *parang*.

Clearing bombs to make way for factories in Jurong

From 1970 to 1988, engineer Tan Suan Yong, 75, helped turn the hills and mosquito-infested swamps of Jurong into Singapore's first industrial estate

One day in the 1970s, I walked into the plywood hut that was my Jurong site office and spotted a shiny little rocket on my colleague's table. He had found it on site. "It's so nice," he said. I froze, having fired something like it during National Service. I said: "Call the Bomb Disposal Unit now!" During World War II, the Japanese attacked Singapore from the west, so in the hillocks of Jurong and Tuas, there were still a lot of their bombs.

I joined JTC (known then as Jurong Town Corporation) on 2 May 1970, and went to the Jurong hills to get to know the terrain, as I needed to consider how to go about levelling them and preparing the land plots for industrialists to build their factories. I would have to get contractors to cut these hills and use the earth to fill the swamps. The hills were the same ones I had run on when I was in NS. But now I had to look at the terrain more closely, I would sometimes see flies in the area and when I poked about there, I would see what resembled human bones. These hills were where you'd find the bodies of those who had been killed by thugs. That, and the many robberies in Jurong, had people calling it the wild, wild west of Singapore. Whenever we found something that seemed human, which was often, we'd call the police. Then we'd have to go out to the main road to lead them in.

In those days, the EDB (Economic Development Board) was active in getting companies such as oil giant Mobil to invest here. Once EDB got them in, it would hand the industrialists over to JTC, which would then prepare plots of land or factory units for them, depending on their requirements. At that time, JTC staff – even its chairman – worked in three-room HDB flats in Jalan Peng Kang, now Corporation Road. The most senior officers occupied the bedrooms, with files all over the place. As Jurong had few telephone lines, they'd knock a hole in the wall so three officers could share a phone. Engineers like me sat in the kitchen when not on site.

JTC also had resettlement officers who had to clear the hills of squatters, most of whom were farmers. Once, I could not wait for one to be compensated for the loss of his pigsty and rambutan and guava trees, because the process would take up to nine months. So I said: "All I want is to cut a small road through your farm. My resettlement colleagues will prepare a document to certify that we will compensate you." He agreed. On the appointed day, I was there with the contractor and his bulldozer. The squatter, all sunburnt and burly, was sitting in front of his house, slowly sharpening his *parang* (machete). I said: "We agreed you would move out today." He eyeballed me and said in Hokkien: "*An chwa?* (so what?)" If we angered him, he might chop us. So we said: "OK. We'll get the Finance Department to give you the money fast, and come back another day."

I grew up rearing chickens in a *kampung* in Upper Serangoon, so I was like one of the squatters. Dirt and dust were no strangers to me. My father died when I was 12, and I was second in a family of nine. When I started work at JTC, I earned $650, just a little more than what I pay my maid now. But I could buy a 1200cc Datsun car for $5,000 and my first HDB flat in Lorong 6 Toa Payoh for $7,000.

In my days at JTC, loyalty was paramount; we were all *pak si buay zhao* (we'll stand our ground, even to the death). When we saw what we did actually shaping up, that was satisfaction. I also kept telling myself: "One day, I will be able to tell my grandchildren all this."

Klang-born JY Pillay was chairman of SIA from 1972 to 1996. The chemical engineer now chairs the Council of Presidential Advisers. Recently, the Pope made him a director of the Vatican's financial regulator.

Photo by NG SOR LUAN

SIA took off because other carriers were sleepy

Former Singapore Airlines chairman JY Pillay, 81, talks about the pride and competence that helped put the national carrier on the route to success and international acclaim

The government appointed me co-chairman of Malaysia-Singapore Airlines (MSA) just before it split into SIA and Malaysia Airlines in 1972. The government told SIA: "Don't come back to us for money. You either survive on your own or fold up."

But the management and staff of MSA, and then SIA, were actually very competent. They had a lot of pride in their airline and themselves, and were confident they could do it. They were technically right up there, too, because they had served long apprenticeships with British Airways and Qantas, then the leading carriers.

You could say SIA was very aggressive. It did not have too much regional competition because most airlines were government-owned and so whenever they lost money, their governments would foot the bill. SIA did well by pinching their traffic – becoming expert at picking passengers up in one country, having them transit in a second country and then carrying all of them to a third country.

The Western airlines had other fish to fry as SIA wasn't competing with them in any of their main markets. So SIA had the regional field to itself, and grew about 30 per cent a year for almost two decades.

The other carriers in the region were either sleepy, government-owned or not as proficient as we were operationally. What upset our regional competitors most was that SIA was able to undercut them while offering its customers better-quality service. So people said: "Why should I travel on other airlines?"

Cathay Pacific was good, but it was timid. SIA was the first among Southeast Asian carriers to buy the big Boeing 747s in the 1970s. In 1978, SIA made the Sale of the Century, buying 19 Boeings totalling $900 million. That helped SIA make its mark globally too, as we were not well-known in those days. After that, Cathay very gingerly bought wide-bodied aircraft too, but even then, they were smaller ones such as the McDonnell Douglas DC-10s.

In all this, SIA didn't have a big signboard saying: "This is our vision: To be the biggest airline" or whatever. It was more interested in its values and culture; its principal goal was to satisfy the customer as best as it could, while making a decent surplus so that it could continue to expand and serve the customer. That was good enough fuel to drive it for quite a few decades.

SIA also had very good people in marketing, and Ian Batey for its advertising. He was a genius. Besides creating the Singapore Girl, he advised SIA not to chop and change its brand. I don't know too much about brands and, in SIA, I hardly interfered with the advertising. Sometimes, I would point out: "Your grammar doesn't sound good." But that was all.

The global oil crisis and domestic inflation in the mid-1970s gave us a sobering hangover. But we were confident that, eventually, the market would recover and that we would be able to hold our own. Our costs, especially wages, were much lower then, and so we could continue to grow rapidly.

Today, you've got budget carriers, and the Gulf carriers, which don't have to worry about where the money comes from. So SIA really has to sweat. Its wage bill has gone up, and it has so much competition that it's caught almost in a vice.

SIA is still regarded as one of the world's best carriers, as it keeps winning all the awards. That will continue, and that's the right motive, because SIA achieved that status and distinction through a very long and arduous process – and it is not going to give that up.

Do you know the *satay* man? He's moved

Ngalirdjo Mungin, 94, started hawking *satay* on the streets. Like thousands of other hawkers,
he moved to a stall in a food centre in the early 1970s, which is now operated by one of his sons

The first food I started selling in 1945 was Indonesian *kuih*. That was all I knew how to make. But I wanted to sell *satay* – the problem was, I didn't know how to make it. I was young and too scared to ask anyone, but I stayed in the Sultan Gate area with many other Javanese who sold *satay* so I would just stand near these other *satay*-sellers and memorise the ingredients. At first, I copied them, but after a while, I made changes. Many would use hammers to beat the meat to tenderise it, but I learnt to do everything by hand. It took hours to rub the marinade in, but I felt it was better.

So after four months, I started selling *satay* at 97 Jalan Sultan. Almost every evening, I would walk from there up to Jalan Besar, where there was a football stadium. There were already four or five people selling *satay* there, and we all had our unofficial locations. I would go to the back entrance – everyone knew that belonged to me. Eventually, I also started selling *satay* near the Padang, and in the Bugis and Geylang areas.

It was really hard work. I usually came home around 2 or 3am and then woke up at 5am to go to my day job assisting land surveyors from the Public Works Department. While I was at work in the morning, my wife would prepare the *satay*. Then I would go home, get the *satay*, and start selling at around 2pm till about 2am. At that hour, it was mostly taxi drivers buying from me.

My boss found out I was leaving work early to sell *satay*, but I argued that as a daily-rated worker, I was earning only $4 a day and had 11 mouths to feed, so I needed two jobs. He agreed to let me keep doing it. Through selling *satay*, I could earn around $8 a day.

When I first started selling *satay*, it cost two cents a stick. Then every few years I would have to increase the price, because the price of chicken was also increasing. One stick of satay increased to three cents, then five cents, then 10. Sometimes I would receive bulk orders, mainly from engineers from the Tanjong Pagar area, normally for around 200 sticks. Back then, selling 100 sticks a day was more than enough.

At one point, I tried to set up a stall under the Merdeka Bridge, but the Ministry of Health stopped me. I moved into this stall in Sims Place Food Centre in 1973, when the government started asking hawkers to move off the streets. I knew the man in charge of the Sims Place market, and he asked me to set up shop here. By then, everyone in this area knew me, so he convinced me to move in here, to make it easier for people to come to one location. It was actually a blessing, because after I moved here, I made a lot more. My earnings doubled, then tripled. I could afford to perform the Haj pilgrimage the first year. After that, that's how I would judge if I had made enough – if I had enough to go on the Haj, then I knew I had made enough that year. At that time, it cost around $1,000 to do the pilgrimage.

I started selling less *satay*, and more of other Malay food. I personally prefer doing *satay*, but my wife was a great cook, and made very good *mee soto* and *mee rebus*. When I first started, there were other stalls in this food centre that tried to sell the same things as me, but none lasted.

My stall is named after my wife, Kamisah Dadi, who died in 2010. I actually wanted to name it after myself and register the licence in my name, but I was still doing that other job when I first got the stall and didn't want to get into trouble. As a civil servant, I was not allowed to apply for a licence to own a stall.

About 10 years ago, I passed the stall on to one of my sons. I'm willing to hand down my stall only to my own blood. This place is not about profit. I could easily have sold my dishes for a lot more, but I just looked at the price of meat and vegetables and priced my dishes according to that.

I still come in every day to my stall and eat a bowl of *mee rebus* or *mee soto*. This way I can ensure my son is doing a decent job, that the quality is still good.

At 94, Ngalirdjo Mungin still goes to his stall, which his son runs now, to check if the quality of the *mee rebus* and *mee soto* is still good.

From Queensway to Capitol Theatre for 50 cents

Taxi driver Teo Kim Swee, 75, who used to drive a pirate taxi,
recounts the days of six strangers riding together in a $1,000 car

Photo from TEO KIM SWEE

When I first started driving a pirate taxi in 1968 at the age of 28, I had to be on a constant lookout for police cars. As soon as they appeared in my rear-view mirror, I would speed off, make a loop and return to the same spot where I had parked to wait for customers.

This daily cat-and-mouse game was part of life as a pirate taxi driver, ferrying passengers around without a government-issued licence.

It was not that I did not want to get a licence – I tried applying for one but could not get it. Although I was never caught, my business partner was not so lucky. The government confiscated the grey Isuzu we shared 50-50.

I bought another Isuzu on my own for $1,000, and tried again. I was determined to make a living as a taxi driver, because I enjoyed driving and liked the freedom of not having to answer to anyone but myself. Before then, I had worked as a grocery store delivery man, and as a coffee powder hawker.

I drove my new taxi by night, and by day I worked as a hawker. I balanced both jobs until 1976, when I could earn enough to feed my family by driving alone, bringing in about $600 a month. I had a wife and four children, and lived in a four-room flat in Jurong West.

Pirate taxis then plied fixed routes, like buses do today. My most common route began at Queensway, and went through Orchard Road and Bras Basah Road before ending by Capitol Theatre. Passengers paid 50 cents to ride the entire route, and 30 cents if they alighted halfway.

Taxis then were not a luxury but the most efficient way to get home at a time when there were few buses. It was common for five or six people – all strangers – to pile into my non-air-conditioned car and ride together. The drives would be quiet as no one made small talk.

The roads were also much narrower compared to today, and there were no expressways. But there were also fewer cars, so it did not take too long to get from one place to another.

I got my official licence in 1971, when the government began clamping down on pirate taxis. I had to attend lessons at night for two weeks before taking a road test. I passed. This was also when we made the transition from fixed fares to metered fares.

Driving a taxi in Singapore today is so different. We now drive people from door to door, but there are so many new condominiums popping up that it is hard for us to keep track!

My last day as a taxi driver will be on 30 June 2015, the day before I turn 75, the official retirement age for taxi drivers.

Uneducated folk like me – I received only four years of primary school education – never thought that Singapore would be like it is today. For that, I am very satisfied and feel very fortunate to be Singaporean.

Comfort Delgro taxi driver Teo Kim Swee has been driving a taxi for 47 years. He is seen here in Queensway, near where he used to pick up his passengers, and (on facing page) with a Nissan Cedric taxi in 1980.

Photo by WANG HUI FEN

I sold cars to presidents

In a sign of women's changing roles, Rosie Ang, 77, the first woman car salesman, took on a man's job and stayed on for 53 years

President Benjamin Sheares summoned me to the Istana after my boss sold him a car in the early 1970s. He said: "Rosie, you tell your boss to please rectify the problem because the car keeps stalling." But I didn't mind being scolded because I got to see his office in the Istana – so nice!

Mr Sheares was not the only president I met in my career. Asia Motor, which I joined in 1958, also sold a Peugeot to our first president, Yusof Ishak. I delivered the car to him at the Istana, too. And SR Nathan bought a Mazda, before he became president.

When I left school, my father, who was an assistant to the managing director at Borneo Motors, suggested I join him there as a stenographer, but I thought that would be so boring. Then I saw an ad for a sales representative at Asia Motor. I was 20 then and already into cars – I had passed my driving test the year before and my Dad bought me a used Hillman convertible.

The person who interviewed me asked if I knew about car engines. I said: "If you give me a chance, I can learn. I also love to meet people, I love to talk, I like to move around, and I drive." I got the job, and stayed on for the next 53 years!

My colleagues were all men, much older and experienced. They were sceptical. After all, I was the first woman car sales rep in Singapore. The men were polite, but didn't really teach me how to sell. I went to the most helpful one and asked if I could listen in when he was closing a sale, and he didn't mind.

Since I was new and didn't have my own pool of customers, I couldn't sit in the showroom and wait for people to come. So I went out to canvass for sales in the diesel Peugeot 403 that the company provided. In my high heels – never courts – I drove everywhere, even to muddy areas in Jurong.

I went to Sembawang, too, to give out my name cards and brochures to the military personnel stationed there. About two weeks into the job, I made my first sale, to a British naval officer. It was a German-made Borgward station wagon costing around $8,000. I was so happy. That was a $30 commission!

My basic pay was $150 a month. It was OK, because back then, $500 could feed a family. I married in my early 20s, and my daughter came along soon after.

My days were long, but my hard work paid off. Being a woman also helped, as some customers may have pitied me. My average was four new cars and four used cars a month, which compared quite well with my colleagues.

In 1964, we brought in Mazda, but people didn't trust a Japanese make. They would say, that's just a Milo tin. But the car proved reliable, and sales soared. I once sold 20 cars at one time to a customer and his group of friends.

Apart from the lull periods when Certificate of Entitlement prices were high and Japanese cars became expensive, work life was mainly a breeze. I had plenty of referrals. The important things were integrity and punctuality. You also had to follow up with your customers, but yet not be a nuisance.

These were guidelines I passed on to my sales team too when I was made a manager around 1970. But after 20 years of that, I decided to go back into front-line sales again. I wanted more time for myself, and it was easier just having to make the sales numbers. And I did, getting the top sales award for the 2004-2005 and 2007-2008 financial years. When Mazda Motor was taken over by another agency in 2011, I decided to call it a day. I was then 73, and I also stopped driving.

But I still love cars, and will spend more than an hour washing my daughter's car. The only part I don't clean is the engine – I don't want to dirty my nails!

ASIA MOTOR CO., LTD.

亞洲嘜哆有限公司

Veteran car sales representative Rosie Ang, at the back of her company's car showroom in Ngee Ann Building in Orchard Road, in the 1960s. The showroom was one of several in the Orchard area, and had been there since 1956. In 1964, the agency was renamed Mazda Motor.

Photo from ROSIE ANG

All at the same level
at the negotiation table

Veteran union leader Abdul Rahman Mahbob, 76, was inspired to get a fair deal
for workers, when, as a clerk, he saw a strike. Today, things are much more peaceful

I was driven to join the union by a very big strike in 1966 by the Public Daily-Rated Employees' Union. They had a fiery president called Suppiah. There were about 15,000 daily-rated employees. When he fought for better pay, he was rejected. Then they decided to go on strike – at that time, the law had not been passed yet that essential services unions cannot go on strike. I was a clerk at Pasir Panjang power station, and I was not involved.

The union members went on strike at the gates of the power stations. For our safety, the company took the rest of us by boat from Clifford Pier to the power station jetty, accompanied by police. We went in by the back gate. It dawned on me that the protesters were not educated people, but they were striking for their salaries to be raised, to get what they felt they deserved. And it struck me – why should there be a difference between daily-rated and monthly staff? We were all working together. That made me want to join the union, and help workers get a fair deal.

I rose through the ranks. I became a committee member, and when the city council was reorganised and called the Public Utilities Board (PUB), I became assistant secretary and then vice-president of the PUB Staff Union. In 1995, when PUB corporatised, the electricity and gas departments went to Singapore Power. We formed a new union, UPAGE, Union of Power and Gas Employees, and I was elected president.

We found a lot of apprehension on the ground. The thinking of workers was, what do we get if the union works with the management? So we talked to every branch and depot, to explain it was to their advantage to work with management.

The most critical negotiation was in 2003 or 2004, when Senoko Power Station management proposed to retrench more than 140 workers. Technology had made many jobs redundant. We had to convince management that certain people should be kept. So we made a study of each individual's work performance, gave it to management. Then we negotiated, pointing out why the number was too high. We managed to come down to 100 – so more than 40 people were saved from being retrenched. Then we negotiated for a better retrenchment package – not just one month's pay for one year of service. They agreed to 110 per cent of each month's salary for every year worked, plus $2,500 for training and upgrading.

It's not easy to see men cry. There were more retrenchments in 2004 at Pulau Seraya Power Station. The ones who were not retrenched cried the hardest because they were crying for their friends. Those retrenched got their cheque and left, but there was this quiet Malay guy, who just sat in a corner. They called in a counsellor, who said to me: "You don't come in, this is my job. I'll convince him." I waited for 1½ hours, then knocked on the door. I told the counsellor: "Look, why don't you go out for a while? Let me handle him, he's my member." I told the man straight: "This is not going to be the end of the world for you." He had a wife and two kids and he was the sole breadwinner, that's why it was so difficult for him. I said: "What I can do is try my best to see if I can get you a job in some other company under our union."

The next day I rang up the Singapore Power CEO and said: "This man is in a desperate state. He needs a job badly and his record is not bad." Just 20 minutes later he called to say that Power Gas had a job for him.

When I first joined, the unions were quite militant. In the beginning, management and workers were more antagonistic in their negotiations, but now we work together. Workers understand that they play a part in being able to remain in their jobs, and management is more prepared to share information. Whenever there is a change in company top management, I tell them: "When we sit at this table across from each other to negotiate, I am no longer your office boy and you are no longer the president. When we sit here, we are at the same level."

In negotiations, no matter how hard management might try to be, no matter how egoistic, you remain calm. Follow the willow – the harder the wind, the more it bends, and finally the wind has to give up. And you stand back up.

Abdul Rahman Mahbob once sent a retrenched worker home because he thought the man was in no state of mind to ride his motorcycle. The very next day, he got him a new job.

She came from China as a maid and stayed on, and on

Domestic helper Kwan Chan Yong, 85, has been with the same family for 60 years.
A Singaporean now, she has been working here since coming from China as a teen

I left China for Singapore when I was 16 years old. The journey in 1946 by sea took a week, and I kept throwing up because of the tossing waves. My aunt and I were travelling third class. We didn't have cabins and had to sleep on canvas beds on the deck.

My aunt, who was already teaching in Singapore, had gone back for me as my father's furniture shop had been destroyed in the war.

I went to work as a domestic helper for an Indonesian Chinese family who dealt in coffee and other commodities in a big office near Lau Pa Sat. The family stayed upstairs, and I would sweep the floor for two hours as there were six rooms. But laundry was worse – I had to wash 11 people's clothes, in the morning and at night, using a washing board and bars of yellow soap cut from longer blocks.

The pay of $40 a month was not bad, but I left after four months because the other worker there ignored me and I had no friends. After that I found work with a doctor and then a cigarette distributor, who had a big bungalow.

But housework was nothing compared to my job as a cook for about 40 Malaysian student boarders at The Chinese High School dormitory. I had to draw water from a well for cooking, and even chop firewood for the stove.

Then, in 1954, when I was 24 years old, I joined the Yeoh family as a domestic helper and have been with them ever since. The husband and wife were both doctors, with an 18-month-old daughter and a month-old son. Although this was my first time looking after children, I didn't find it hard.

When the boy was 13, he went to London to study. My employers wanted me to keep him company for a month before his term started. It was my first time on a plane – it was such a long journey – and again I kept throwing up. In London we visited Buckingham Palace and No. 10 Downing Street, took boat rides and rode the trains. It was fun.

After my employer's daughter got married, she also studied in Britain, doing her post-grad studies for about four years. And as her newborn daughter was with her, again I went there to help. It was difficult looking after the baby during winter. She had to be wrapped up in many layers and when she dirtied herself, it was a struggle to undo her clothes and clean her. When it got too cold for me and my fingers were splitting and my nose bleeding, I came back. But a few months later I would go again. So I went to and from there several times.

My life nowadays is more placid. I still travel with the family now, but for holidays. I have my own room with a TV, fan and air-conditioner. There are three other maids here and they share a room.

My main responsibilities are to cook and do the marketing. About twice or three times a week I go to the Tiong Bahru, Tekka or Ghim Moh market, depending on what I need. The driver takes me there, and he helps me carry my purchases. When I first joined the family, there was no driver; I took a bus to the market, and it was a 20-minute walk home from the bus stop. A couple of times it flooded and I struggled to carry the stuff on my back – they also didn't use many plastic bags then and things wrapped in newspapers would get wet.

After so many years, I'm very fond of the family – the children call me Ah Por, which means grandmother – and my employer's daughter is still attached to me. I'll tell you how attached. In 2010, my relatives in China who are now rich – I used to send them money and also food like legs of ham – asked me to return to our hometown of Dongguan. They thought it was time I led a comfortable life back in China. They bought a flat for me, and a maid came to do the housework. But my employer's daughter kept calling me, asking me to come back to Singapore. Well, there was nothing much to do in the flat all by myself, and there're people here who consider me family too, so after six months, I came back!

Along the way, with this family, I have become a very good cook, a fussy cook. Once I let one of the maids help me cut chillies. Some slices were big, some small – so ugly! So I do everything now. I can try a dish once and know how to recreate it. If you have the heart to learn something, you will remember it, because I can't write things down as I never went to school.

I'm still healthy, except my right vision isn't very good. I've been here for 60 years because I've been happy working here. I can't say what will happen in the future, but I pass my days happily now.

Kwan Chan Yong, considered by her employer's family as a living treasure, cooks up a storm when there are guests. She is fastidious in the kitchen and removes even the bones of the little *ikan bilis* in her *nasi lemak*.

Pioneering diplomat and former journalist Lee Khoon Choy represented Singapore in seven countries over 20 years. The former minister and MP for Bukit Panjang, Hong Lim and Braddell Heights retired from politics in 1988.

I slept with a pistol under my pillow

Lee Khoon Choy, 91, was the man Singapore entrusted
with its most delicate diplomatic missions in its early years

One morning in 1968, I got a call from Foreign Minister S Rajaratnam. He said: "Singapore is going to recognise Israel as a nation and the Arabs are going to be angry. We need somebody in Egypt to pacify them. You are the only one who can do it." I said: "No. I'm a politician, not a diplomat."

At that time, I was the Minister of State for Culture, and had many plans to develop the arts. I'd been Mr Rajaratnam's parliamentary secretary when he was Minister for Culture earlier. I'd also raised funds to build the National Theatre.

Then Prime Minister Lee Kuan Yew called me. I'd been his political secretary from 1963 to 1965 and I found him frank, most courageous and a very good strategist. Mr Lee said: "KC, we want you to do a job – and you must do it." I told him that my two sons from my late first wife were about to enter secondary school, and there wouldn't be anyone to look after them if my second wife and I went to Egypt. But he insisted and that was that.

I got my sister-in-law to care for my sons, and left for Egypt with my second wife and our three daughters. My job, in one sentence, was "to ensure that when Singapore recognised Israel, our embassies would not burn".

Once in Cairo, I made friends with the ambassadors there. British ambassador Harold Beeley became a close friend, translating Arab newspapers for me regularly. I learnt that the Arabs had no objections to Singapore recognising Israel's sovereignty, as long as we also supported United Nations resolutions that Israel should not occupy Arab territories. That is what Singapore did. So it was that I finished my job there well.

I think my personality helped; I like mixing with people and, wherever I go, I make it a point to study the real culture of a country, from how its people behave to why they do what they do. Wherever I went, I also kept in touch with cultural leaders, be they singers or painters. Diplomacy also came to me naturally, perhaps because as a boy I had to mediate between my father's two wives and my 10 brothers and four sisters. I was the seventh son of Lee Kim Fook, once the richest man in Penang.

In Egypt, I was also ambassador to four other countries – Ethiopia, Lebanon, Yugoslavia and Pakistan. This was because the government did not have much money at that time; I worked on five countries for about $2,000 a month. Fortunately, the government provided housing and education for my family. But when I became ambassador to Japan in 1984, I had to pay for the education of my three daughters, who were studying at Sophia University there, as they were older than 18. Luckily, when I was ambassador to Indonesia in the 1970s, I'd bought a Japanese vase for $7,000. When someone in Japan saw that vase, he said

it was very rare and paid me $250,000 for it, which covered all my daughters' tertiary fees!

Being ambassador to Indonesia from 1970 to 1974 was tough. Despite pleas from Indonesia, Singapore had in 1968 hanged two of its marines for killing three people when they bombed MacDonald House here in 1965. Still, after three years, I succeeded in persuading the Indonesian government to invite Mr Lee to Indonesia.

Then, two men on a motorcycle came to my house in Jakarta and handed me a letter. It said that if I did not get the Singapore government to change its policies which were friendly to the Chinese, they would not be responsible for my body, or those of my three embassy staff. Fortunately, my wife and children were back in Singapore. I flew home and asked Mr Rajaratnam for a bodyguard, but he said: "We are a small country; we cannot afford that."

So I went to Thomson Police Station and practised shooting with a pistol. When I returned to Jakarta, I went to see my friend General Widodo, the city's commissioner of police. I told him: "Anybody who threatens to shoot me, I'll shoot first." He said: "Don't do that. I'll give you the name of someone to call if anything happens." I thought: "What would be the use of names when somebody shoots me?" There were cocktail parties every night at the many embassies in Jakarta, and I took my pistol with me to these parties, looking around all the time for anyone who made a move. At night, I slept with the pistol under my pillow.

Nothing happened, and I told my wife about the threat only after I'd left Indonesia in 1974. After that, I returned to politics here and also helped Singapore develop its relations with China.

From 1984 till I retired in 1988, I was the ambassador to Japan and South Korea. I had spent the last two years of World War II bowing to a picture of Emperor Hirohito every morning with my students, to whom I was teaching the Japanese language. I didn't know then that, 40 years later, I would be bowing and presenting my credentials to that very emperor. My wife and I were invited to lunch once with Emperor Hirohito, as was the custom among envoys there. I asked him which period of his 60-year reign he liked best, and he replied: "It was in 1921, when I visited Singapore on my way to Europe. I went to the Botanic Gardens; it was beautiful."

I've always had strong stamina and I don't give up easily. After I'd been ambassador to Indonesia for about two years, Deputy Premier Goh Keng Swee said: "KC, don't waste your time, they won't invite Mr Lee to visit them. Come home." But I stayed on because whatever I start, I must finish well.

Singapore's first Prime Minister and founding father Lee Kuan Yew was instrumental in shaping the country's history. He was also one of the world's longest-serving premiers, his term from 1959 to 1990 running for 31 years and 176 days.

Photo from LEE KUAN YEW

Singaporeans were in no mood to crawl back

Photo by FRANCIS ONG

The nation succeeded in its first decade because its people were determined to do well on their own after separating from Malaysia, said Singapore's first Prime Minister, Lee Kuan Yew, 91*

I did not expect that at the age of 42 I would be in charge of an independent Singapore, responsible to better the lives of two million people.

We were turfed out of Malaysia for pressing for equal rights for non-*bumiputras*. Many believed we could not survive without a hinterland. They expected us to fail and to crawl back to Malaysia on their terms. It did not happen. The people of Singapore decided to make a go of independence, which was thrust upon them.

At the time, my thoughts were of having let down the people in Singapore and Malaya who believed in a multiracial society with the different races having equal opportunities and working together. But the bitter experience we had in the two years in Malaysia when we were made to feel like second-class citizens strengthened our resolve to succeed on our own. The people in Singapore were in no mood to crawl back.

It was hard going at first because we had so few assets. But the key to our survival was confidence. We had confidence in ourselves and created the conditions for Singapore to succeed. We trained our people, put in place infrastructure and developed a cohesive society.

Slowly but surely, companies, especially multinational ones, began to see a stable and efficient Singapore as a place in which to invest. It was an outcome beyond expectations, especially to the Malayans who expected us to go back on their terms.

We made it because of the grit and determination of the people to make our country work. The government provided strong leadership because that's the only way for Singapore to excel and secure its future. We were open about the problems and challenges we faced. We didn't shy away from telling the people the harsh realities of succeeding as a nation without any natural resources.

I had concluded early on that the only way Singapore, an island state in Southeast Asia, could survive was to be extraordinary. It could not be ordinary. We had to be better than our neighbours, work harder and be better organised, or they would bypass us and we would lose our role as a middleman and an entrepôt for the region.

The people understood what they were in for and were prepared to make sacrifices.

The progress you see today is the result of hard work and careful planning. It is a team effort.

But we must always remember the basics that have got us here: a socially cohesive society through the fair sharing of the benefits of progress, equal opportunities for all, and meritocracy, with the best man or woman for the job. Then we can better ensure that Singapore continues to achieve happiness, prosperity and progress for our nation, to better the lives of Singaporeans.

* Mr Lee passed away on 23 March 2015

Living in
Early Singapore

Life was simple then but people
knew how to make the most of it

I was about a year old, and sitting in a multi-purpose bamboo stool in this photo taken in April 1972. These stools were popular because, turned on their side, they could be used as a feeding chair for young kids. Standing beside me at our uncle's home is my elder sister Seow Pin, a year older.

Housewife Lock Seow Yen, 43

My friends and I, around 16 or 17 then, loved to visit different places on public holidays like National Day or Labour Day. We would go to places like Haw Par Villa, Changi Beach, Tanjong Rhu and Katong Park to take photos and have picnics by the beach. Here we are at MacRitchie Reservoir in a photo taken around 1966.

Housekeeper Wong Yoke Leng (second from left), 65

That's my friend, Thang Hock Huat (right), 13, and I, 15 at the time. We would visit places of interest frequently. We liked this figure at Haw Par Villa and took a photo in front of it; this was in 1972.

General manager Tian Toh Kian, 58

After our usually early dinner, if the weather was nice, my family would drive down to Kallang Park to take a walk. We three brothers would run and play around this weird futuristic-looking fountain. Watching over us here is our Grandma, who was visiting from Hainan.

Retiree Kevin Guo (left), 58, seen here with younger brother Eddie (in front), elder brother Jimmy and their grandmother

I was thrilled to bits to be out with my other teenage school chums on a planned Chinese New Year outing. In the days of no Internet and fewer distractions, it was a novelty to go out and have fun on Chinese New Year, donning new clothes, eating New Year goodies and visiting different places. Here my classmate Tan Yong Suan and I – we were around 15 or 16 – are sitting on the steps outside Van Kleef Aquarium near Fort Canning.

Communications specialist Sant Kaur, 56

My wife and I used to go to the Botanic Gardens almost every weekend during our dating days. This picture was taken in November 1972, just after we got engaged. I was 22 and she was 19. Last time, Singapore was not like today, with so many places to go to and things to do. So we always kept going to the Botanic Gardens to walk around and chit-chat. Sometimes we would take food and have a picnic. We also liked to go to Arab Street to makan, and sometimes we would watch movies at Capitol Theatre or Odeon Theatre. When this picture was taken, I was working for Shell in Pulau Bukom, where I was until I retired a few years ago.

Retiree Abdul Hadi Tairek, 65

My friends and I, aged 21 or 22 then, would go to my relative's hairdressing salon in Joo Chiat because she had a TV, and we would watch wrestling there on Friday or Saturday nights after work. One of my friends was also keen on a girl working there. This photo was taken around 1965 or 1966.

**Security officer
Foo Suan Boon (seated, centre), 71**

My brother and sister and I loved to play with our neighbours in the corridor outside our homes. This photo was taken around the mid-1970s, when we were living at Block 2, Toa Payoh Lorong 7. We were there for about 16 or 17 years.

Navy officer Tay Yew Hui (right), 47, seen here with older sister Pui Lin and brother Chieh Hui.

I can't remember where this is but it must have been around MacRitchie Reservoir or Toa Payoh. I wasn't actually allowed to go out with my friends, so we wouldn't have ventured far from our school, Thomson Secondary. My friend Yuk Ming and I, both 15 then, probably took this picture because we thought the statue was cute – I don't think we had any idea that it was a replica of the famous Manneken Pis in Belgium.

Master teacher Varalackshmi Hariharan, 58

My sister, Choh Hua (left), was here visiting from Malaysia with her five kids, aged from two to eight. My friend (centre) and I took them to visit many places here and ended up at Nanyang University.

Housewife Soh Hui Ngoh, 77

1965 — 1974

1965

- Three people are killed and 33 others injured when two Indonesian saboteurs **bomb MacDonald House** on 10 March. The duo are later convicted and hanged in 1968

- At 10 am on 9 August, a tearful Prime Minister Lee Kuan Yew announces Singapore's **shock separation** from Malaysia; in September, the new republic is admitted as the 117th member of the United Nations

- Swimmer Patricia Chan, 11, becomes **Singapore's Golden Girl** when she wins eight gold medals at the 3rd Southeast Asian Peninsular Games. She wins 31 more golds in four further Games

1966

- Foreign Minister S Rajaratnam drafts the **National Pledge**, which students across the nation recite for the first time on 24 August

- Kandang Kerbau Hospital gets a Guinness world record for delivering the **most babies** – 39,835 in a year. The record stands till 1976

- In May, 1,233,205 residents here get new laminated **identity cards**, pink for citizens and blue for permanent residents

1967

- The newly minted Board of Commissioners of Currency issues **the first Singapore dollar**, with an orchid motif. Its value is at par with the Malaysian ringgit till 1973

- Deputy Prime Minister Goh Keng Swee introduces compulsory **National Service**, beginning with 9,000 or so recruits for the Singapore Armed Forces

- On 8 August, Singapore co-founds the **Association of Southeast Asian Nations** with Malaysia, Indonesia, Thailand and the Philippines to keep the region peaceful

1968

- The People's Action Party sweeps all 58 seats in Singapore's first post-Independence **general election**, which the opposition Barisan Sosialis boycotts

- The first **Arts Festival** is held, marking the progress of multicultural integration in multiracial Singapore

- **Toto** debuts here as Singapore's first legalised lottery, giving punters a chance to win up to $500,000

1969

- A unit of **female volunteer soldiers**, including teachers, clerks and nurses in their 20s, is formed. They are taught how to march and shoot

- **Long-haired men are barred** from entering the country, and Singaporean men who persist with Beatles-style hair risk losing jobs and university places

- Three die in Singapore's **worst floods** in 35 years; three-quarters of the island are deluged in December, with water, electricity and telephone services disrupted

Singapore separates from Malaysia and begins its journey as an independent nation

1970

- The government begins clearing the streets and **resettling 25,000 itinerant hawkers** in food centres over five years

- Singapore conducts its first **Census of the Population** post-Independence

- Housewife Doreen Tan undergoes Singapore's **first kidney transplant**; the donor is 20-year-old Yee Kwok Tong

1971

- Gynaecologist **Benjamin Sheares** becomes the second president, after Yusof Ishak's death on 23 November 1970

- **Britain withdraws** the last of its 15,000 troops here, leaving 17,000 locals jobless

- Gynaecologist and in-vitro fertilisation pioneer SS Ratnam performs Singapore's **first sex change operation** successfully on a 24-year-old man

1972

Small Families Brighter Future

Two is enough

- The government introduces the contentious **Stop At Two** population control policy

- The **National Wages Council**, chaired by economist Lim Chong Yah, is formed to moderate matters among employers, trade unions and the government

- Nine people die on 21 November, when a short circuit causes the **Robinsons department store fire.** The 114-year-old building in Raffles Place is reduced to rubble

1973

- The $50 million **National Stadium** in Kallang opens in July. In September the 55,000-seat stadium hosts the opening ceremony of the 7th Southeast Asian Peninsular (SEAP) Games, the first international sports event held in Singapore

- Prime Minister Lee Kuan Yew opens the first **National Trades Union Congress Welcome supermarket** in Toa Payoh. It sells affordable basic necessities

- An oil embargo causes jitters and the **loss of $1 billion** from the fledgling Singapore Stock Exchange on 26 November

1974

- Singaporeans welcome the new year in darkness because of the **worst blackout** since World War II

- Four armed men **hijack the ferry *Laju*,** after trying to bomb Pulau Bukom earlier. No one is injured and the men are later granted safe passage out of Singapore

- **Pianist Seow Yit Kin**, 19, is named one of London's most outstanding musicians by the Greater London Arts Association

- Singaporeans enjoy the **World Cup final "live"** and in colour for the first time. West Germany beat Holland 2-1

A NATION FINDS ITS FEET

There is nothing like sport, and football especially, to galvanise a young nation. In May 1977, Singapore celebrates winning the Malaysia Cup after 12 years. Doing a lap of honour after the team beat Penang 3-2 in Kuala Lumpur are (front row, from left) Lim Teng Sai, Edmund Wee, V Khanisen and Zainal Abidin.

Photo from THE STRAITS TIMES

Chief bus captain Elizabeth Lim Poh Suan in her purple uniform, adopted in 2013. When she first started out, her company's uniform was blue (top photo, facing page, taken in 1984). The colour was changed in 2000 to green, in the bottom photo, taken in 2011.

Photo by DESMOND FOO

Passengers carried live chickens onto my bus

Elizabeth Lim Poh Suan, 57, the highest-ranking female bus driver at
SBS Transit, has seen the days of manual transmission and no air-conditioning

In 1981 I was a factory worker when I spotted an advertisement for bus drivers and conductors for Singapore Bus Service (SBS). I had always admired bus drivers for their ability to handle large vehicles, and wanted to try my hand at it.

On 23 July that year, at the age of 22, I became a certified bus driver after obtaining a licence to drive heavy vehicles. I had considered applying to be a bus conductor, but my mother did not like the idea of me, a woman, squeezing through a crowded bus.

Driving a bus was a really tough job. The engine was noisy; it had a manual transmission with a double clutch; and there was no power steering. My arms became very strong. There was no air-conditioning, which made for very warm bus rides.

Buses then were quite different from buses today, which are air-conditioned and have automatic transmissions. We also had to maintain the bus daily, such as topping up the radiator water and brake oil. Now mechanic colleagues maintain the buses.

My usual route on Bus 179 began at Bukit Timah, where Beauty World Centre is today, and ended in Lim Chu Kang. There were only army camps and farms there, and the farmers would board in their rubber boots, T-shirts and shorts. Some would even carry live chickens in cages. Children would often be in old, used clothes, unlike young ones today who wear new, branded clothing.

At each stop, the bus conductor would wait for all passengers to board – the bus had only one door, at the centre – and then tap the ceiling with his ticket puncher to signal to the driver to move off. During the ride, the conductor would collect fares and issue tickets. SBS, now SBS Transit, switched to two-door buses in 1984, when it also phased out bus conductors.

Drivers perform well by driving safely, providing good customer service and having a good record of attendance. Although my industry is male-dominated – there are fewer than 400 women out of 5,800 drivers – both men and women can do well. This is why I have stayed on for so long. There are also some advantages to being a woman in this job. When the bus breaks down, or its engine needs to be topped up with water, my male colleagues are quick to offer help. I have also had my fair share of admirers, but I always tell them I am married. I married my husband, a cement mixer driver, in 1978. We have two daughters aged 22 and 36 and four grandchildren between the ages of eight and 18.

Most bus captains, as drivers are referred to now, are familiar with about five routes each, but I have about 40 routes, picked up over 32 years of driving. I am also a mentor to other bus captains, and train them regularly. Thankfully, I have had a clean driving record for 30 years.

Photos from
ELIZABETH LIM
POH SUAN

When I was told in 2011 that I was going to be made the only female chief bus captain, the highest rank for a bus driver, I was so happy I was even smiling in my sleep! My daughter told me: "Mummy, I feel proud of you!"

I plan on doing this until I retire at the age of 70. The retirement age for bus drivers is 67, and contracts can be offered to those who are deemed fit to drive. As long as I am healthy, I will work.

Alan Choe was Singapore's first urban planner and, in his time, gave architects greater exposure and more work by requiring developers to submit architectural designs in their tenders.

I unleashed a building boom

Architect Alan Choe, 84, was Singapore's first urban planner. During his time, prime land
was sold to private developers to build malls and skyscrapers, transforming the skyline

In 1961, I was headhunted to join the Housing Board (HDB) as Singapore's first town planner. By then, the government had vowed to build a total of 50,000 flats within five years to resettle slum-dwellers. The job fell to me. Now, how would I complete that many flats in such a short time? To begin with, doing so would change human density here greatly, to about 600 people per acre. Second, I'd first have to clear squatters off all available land. Third, I'd have to build the flats in fairly central areas. Fourth, the government had little money then.

By 1965, my team and I at the HDB had completed 54,430 flats, by building mostly one-room units and using cement blocks which were bigger, lighter and cheaper than bricks. Construction was cruising along by 1963, such that the government asked me to look into clearing Singapore of slums, to improve further the quality of life here. By then, four visiting experts in town planning had concluded that Singapore was ready for urban renewal, which is about redeveloping highly sought-after downtown locations in ways which maximise land value. So the HDB had me head its new urban renewal team.

At that time, Orchard Road was already the place to see and be seen. Some of the landmarks along this 2.2km boulevard were CK Tang, the largest Chinese-style building that was not a temple, Singapore's most important car showrooms, Mont d'Or coffeehouse and Peranakan-style houses. But its best attraction was the open-air carpark where Orchard Central is today. At night, hawkers converged there and turned it into Glutton's Square, whose lights, smells and flavours were magnets for locals and tourists alike. All this came about largely without government intervention.

But also running along Orchard Road then, on the side where Ngee Ann City is today, was a big, open canal. I saw that as a great waste of prime land, and so decided to cover the entire canal up, as doing so would increase Orchard Road's span by more than a third. After much debate in the Cabinet, I got the go-ahead to cover up Orchard Canal.

My HDB boss wanted to build flats downtown. I argued that the land there would be better used for projects that developed Singapore's economy. The government broke this impasse in 1974, by spinning off my department as an autonomous statutory board, which is now known as the Urban Redevelopment Authority. At that time, the only big buildings here were The Cathay in Handy Road and the Asia Insurance Building in Robinson Road. The private sector then had neither the initiative nor the means to buy large land plots, clear them of squatters and build on them. My colleagues and I discussed with the Economic Development Board as well as businesspeople here what exactly was needed for Singapore to grow fast. When I heard what they had to say, I realised that I'd have to partner the private sector to redevelop downtown Singapore.

So I told the government that it needed to do three things for urban renewal to work here: First, reduce property tax to 20 per cent to encourage the private sector to redevelop sites here; second, allow private developers to pay for land in easy instalments as few could cough up money to buy land; and third, approve developers' building plans quickly and smoothly.

I jumped for joy when the government reduced property tax to 12 per cent and allowed developers here to pay for the land over 20 years. Without all those incentives, it would have been a struggle for Singapore to go from Third World to First in the time it did.

My first site sale, comprising three plots meant for hotels at Havelock Road, created a buzz for the area. Emboldened by that, I decided to sell five sites at one shot for the development of five office towers that collectively became Shenton Way. Up till then, Raffles Place was a key commercial area but people there still worked out of old shophouses, with their files piled along creaky staircases.

After Shenton Way was a success, we cleared Beach Road of its old theatres, including the Alhambra, and created the hotel-and-office stretch to which I gave the auspicious name Golden Mile, to attract investors.

Our sales of sites scheme also led to the rejuvenation of Orchard Road, but this meant that even the popular Glutton's Square had to make way for malls.

Tan Gee Paw, who enjoys painting water scenes in his spare time, was asked to draw up the plan to clean up the Singapore and Kallang rivers in 1977. The clean-up was finished, on target, in 1987.

Photo from PUB, Singapore's national water agency

Miners with missing fingers and their part in the water story

For civil engineer Tan Gee Paw, 71 – chairman of PUB since 2001
– increasing Singapore's water supply has been a life-long effort, culminating in NEWater

I studied civil engineering at the University of Malaya in Kuala Lumpur on a government bursary, and so had a four-year bond to serve upon graduation, at the Public Works Department (PWD) here. Its director Hiew Siew Nam got me to maintain drains here. I was quite downhearted at first. But then I became fascinated with the network of drains, canals and rivers here, especially as I enjoyed painting water scenes in my spare time. Then, between 1971 and 1973, I was put in charge of the $6.7 million Bukit Timah flood alleviation project, in which we had to hack through laterite and rock to build three tunnels to manage floodwater. There were no tunnel borers here then so our contractors got gold miners from Malaysia to hack through laterite with only their *cangkuls* (hoes). These miners were experts at planting dynamite to blast through rock, which they could not hack through. Many among these miners had one or two fingers missing.

After I finished that project, two of my PWD colleagues and I formed the Water Planning Unit in the mid-1970s to forecast Singapore's future demand for water and plan how to meet it. We could see even then that if we could recycle half of all wastewater discharged here, we would not need reservoirs anymore. So, in 1974, we built Singapore's first water recycling plant in Ulu Pandan with the help of the Canadians.

They wanted 100 per cent of the payment upfront before they would do anything for us. The recycled water we produced was clear and met World Health Organisation standards, but the water-filtering membrane technology was then too expensive and unreliable. We had to wait another 25 years for that technology to be cheaper and highly dependable.

Then in 1977, I was asked to draw up the plan to clean up the Singapore and Kallang rivers, and also do a short report to Prime Minister Lee Kuan Yew, to tell him what the clean-up would entail. That was because the project was not only about cleaning up rivers, but also about changing lifestyles. Farmers would have to give up their pigs and fruit trees, move into high-rise flats and work in factories. That might have far-reaching political implications.

Once Mr Lee agreed to the project, we launched a massive programme to provide every household here with a sewer. We focused on Chinatown because waste there went right into the Singapore River. We knew we had broken the back of the water pollution problem when the last nightsoil wagon rolled into Chinatown. I got senior PWD officers to line up along the road to welcome that wagon.

There were two difficult things about the clean-up: One was persuading bumboat operators along the Singapore River either to give up their livelihoods or relocate to Pasir Panjang. When all of them finally left, the river lost its bustle and colour and became totally sterile for a while. The Boat Quay godowns, which these bumboats used to serve, were like ghost houses. The other difficulty was ridding Tanjong Rhu of its shipyards. The Economic Development Board wanted them to stay put as they were good for the economy, so those building Benjamin Sheares Bridge nearby had to put a hump in it to make the bridge higher for ships to pass under safely. That hump caused a traffic bottleneck for years.

It was a relief to finish the clean-up, on target, in 1987. It was not so difficult, really, as we had Mr Lee behind us. So what he said was carried through. Even so, in working with others, one cannot be abrasive and aggressive. Otherwise, they might sabotage you. You need to build bridges with everyone.

In 1998, I returned to the question of recycling water at PUB. We built the first NEWater pilot plant in Bedok – in a container. The turning point came when the recycled water, which was stored in a well, was crystal clear; I'd never seen water that sparkled like that. Building a NEWater plant was like fabricating structures with a Lego set. Knowing how to operate the plant was the challenge. In this, my colleague Harry Seah did a good job of tweaking the plant's components until the water quality was stable and the plant could produce pure water consistently and reliably every day.

The bigger battle with NEWater was really to persuade the government that Singapore could recycle wastewater successfully. How could the government trust anyone who just told them that it could be done? But within three months, I managed to persuade Mr Lee and his ministers that we could do it. After NEWater, the challenge of desalting seawater was chicken feed. Desalting is very expensive, but we had to consider it as an independent water source besides our 17 reservoirs and NEWater, because we can reasonably recycle only up to about 70 per cent of wastewater.

Shot by Botak, the Cop Killer

Abd Rahman Khan Gulap Khan, 65, spent 35 years in the police force – most of it in the CID – attending to anything from homicides to the Hotel New World collapse, in which 33 people died

The worst pain I ever felt in my life was on the night that I got shot. Not from the bullet that grazed my stomach, but from the tetanus jab I had to get later in the hospital. Bullets in those days had lead in them, so if you didn't get the jab within six hours, you might get lead poisoning. I couldn't sleep on my buttocks for three days.

I was shot by this guy we called the Cop Killer in 1973, just two years after I joined the police. He shot and killed a detective over a minor traffic accident in the East Coast and the whole police force was searching for him. The breakthrough came from a robber who told us that among the most notorious robbers in Singapore at that time, the most likely to engage with police when confronted was this man known as Botak.

We managed to trace him to Cavenagh Road Apartments. We used a ruse to get him out. When he came out running, a colleague put him in a headlock, but Botak had already pulled out a gun. I grabbed hold of the gun, a stolen police revolver, and he fired two rounds which burned my palm. A third shot grazed my stomach. We couldn't subdue him, so my colleague shot him twice in the arm, but Botak still wouldn't drop his weapon. Then other colleagues rushed in, and one fired a shot that I felt go past my ear, which hit the gunman in the head. He died 13 minutes later.

Then there was the disaster in 1978, when the Greek tanker *Spyros* exploded in Jurong Shipyard. We spent one solid week in the mortuary, which had only a few refrigerated compartments in which to keep the bodies. But we had 76 bodies, and had to leave them lying around, on the floor, to decompose. I remember we were eating *nasi briyani* at an operating table with the bodies on the floor. We had to take our food there because we couldn't leave, as we were waiting for people to come in to identify the bodies,

and every hour the body changes because of decomposition.

After that, I had to throw away all the clothes I was wearing, including my undergarments, shoes, everything, because it all stank. We wore the same things all week; we didn't change because it would all stink up again, so we had to bear with it – just wash up, brush your teeth, that's it. Even a few days after we were done, when I sat in the bus, people were still holding their noses, because the smell sticks to your skin. You bathe with Dettol, you wash your hair, the stink is still there.

I also still remember the Hotel New World collapse in 1986 clearly because I was attending a briefing that morning at the Police Academy about an islandwide raid on gambling operations. Then we suddenly received a call to report to Serangoon Road immediately. A six-storey building was flattened like a biscuit, right to the ground, all of it down. I couldn't believe it. I was assigned to identify and record all the dead, which turned out to be a total of 33. Nine of the 17 people who survived were rescued that first day. That evening, we switched off all the lights, and asked for total silence – no generators, no engines, not even talking, so rescuers could listen for any signs of life, like people knocking.

The last body taken out was from the basement carpark, about a week later. It was that of an old man who looked like he was asleep. The pathologist said the walls that collapsed on him had been whitewashed recently, and the lime had preserved his body.

In those days, we had to do everything ourselves – we were the photographers, the fingerprint takers, and we searched the bodies. That's the reason why we sometimes felt numb to death. Sometimes, for a moment, we felt pity, that the person died in such a manner. At the end of the day, we would try our best to help the family of the dead by bringing the culprit responsible to justice.

Veteran cop Abd Rahman Khan Gulap Khan, surrounded by his many awards and commendations, was on the front line of investigations into major disasters here.

Ipoh-born Wong Yew Kwan settled here in 1970. He was Commissioner of Parks from 1976 till he retired in 1983 at the age of 50.

Photo by DOMINIC WONG

I pleaded for more money for trees

Tree expert Wong Yew Kwan, 82, was the man Lee Kuan Yew called on to help landscape the city and soften the effects of the emerging concrete jungle

When I became Commissioner of Parks in 1976, I kept writing letters to the Finance Ministry for more money to expand my department. But all I got were terse replies that we needn't expand our greening activities because we'd done our job.

That changed in 1978 after a Garden City Action Committee meeting with Prime Minister Lee Kuan Yew. I had asked for money to lay aeration slabs at the foot of each tree. These slabs are bumpy to walk on, but the slats are vital to helping trees breathe.

Mr Lee lectured me and the other committee members for almost two hours on how to make Singapore greener, and at one juncture, he pointed to Permanent Secretary of Finance George Bogaars and said: "Give them the money to help the trees grow. If I put a polythene bag over your head, you would suffocate." He was helping the meeting understand what would happen to tree roots if they were paved over.

After that meeting, we got up to $40 million a year, compared to about $14 million a year before Mr Lee intervened.

I was able to hire more staff, build more parks and continue Mr Lee's dream of big trees for Singapore. In the early 1960s, he said Singapore had to be industrialised and urbanised to move forward. But these two processes would create a concrete jungle full of heat, which would be uncomfortable for everyone living here. That might also reduce rainfall because this depends on steam rising and then condensing. But if the surroundings are too hot, steam just keeps rising without condensing.

To alleviate this, Mr Lee said, we'd have to plant trees wherever and whenever we could. He said: "Give me shade first to block the sunshine reflecting off buildings and roads and disturbing people. Don't worry about plant colours." So we planted his two choices, angsana and raintree, each about 1.5m from the road edges because he wanted trees to shade roads, too, as well as creepers such as fig ivy, baphia and ixora on the walls of flyovers.

Once, he told me: "I want the void areas under flyovers to be covered in greenery." I said: "Prime Minister, we'd need light and water for that. Shall we use artificial lighting?" He said: "No, that would be wasting energy." In the end, we split each flyover in two so light could stream in through the gap running down the middle to the plants below.

It was the same for the overhead pedestrian bridges. Mr Lee found those ugly so he asked that we plant flowers like bougainvillea on them.

At that 1978 meeting, Mr Lee had also told me: "When the first plane lands at Changi Airport in 1981, I want its passengers to see well-tended gardens and not rank vegetation. The airport and Woodlands are the first impressions visitors have of Singapore, and I don't want bad vegetation to give us a bad name." Permanent Secretary Howe Yoon Chong said: "Prime Minister, you're wasting money." Mr Lee said: "How much do you want for a tree? $2,000? And let's not forget, you may have to spend more money to plant and maintain each tree." That's how pragmatic and intent Mr Lee was on making Singapore green.

Working with him was high-pressured. He did not praise unnecessarily, but would sometimes call us up and say: "That was very well done."

Putting the brakes on traffic jams

As Singapore prospered, more people could afford cars. Congestion became a problem.
Gopinath Menon, 71, who went on to be chief transportation engineer from 1991 to 2001,
recalls the introduction of the system that led to today's electronic road gantries

In 1975, we introduced congestion pricing as the Area Licensing Scheme (ALS). My traffic engineer colleagues and I had considered alternatives, such as imposing high parking fees downtown and number plate rationing where, say, even-numbered cars could be driven downtown only on even-numbered days.

But in the end, we thought congestion pricing the fairest system because drivers paid for actual use of their cars during peak hours. British statistician Reuben Smeed, who taught me when I was doing my Master's in traffic engineering – in Sydney, on a fellowship – was the father of congestion pricing. My colleagues and I talked about his 1962 *Smeed Report* and decided to put it to Prime Minister Lee Kuan Yew. Mr Lee said: "Give me time to think about it." Some time later, he said: "Proceed." Without someone like him to champion it, we could not have done it because, politically, it was dynamite.

We needed more than 150 people to run ALS. Most drivers needed manually issued licences to enter the 720ha Restricted Zone downtown during the rush hour. It became so labour-intensive that ALS went electronic in 1998, as Electronic Road Pricing (ERP).

I enjoyed my work as project director for congestion pricing because we had an almost blank slate to shape Singapore's public and road transportation networks. My boss was the top man in transport then, Lim Leong Geok, eldest son of war hero Lim Bo Seng. He and my other colleagues were prepared to take risks.

Around 1975, I also began working closely with Leslie Wong, Commander of Traffic Police. We were upset to see that most accident victims were pedestrians. We can't afford to lose even one person. So Leslie and I said, this won't do, and that's how we started the whole pedestrian programme. We went full-on in paving over open canals and drains to provide pedestrian walkways, building pedestrian bridges, footpaths and underpasses, and putting up red-man-green-man lights.

I have two regrets. First, we were too fast in putting up the bridges. We thought that if we went for zebra crossings instead, that would slow traffic down. But these bridges are not pedestrian-friendly; each is 5.4m or 40 steps high, which is all right for the young but not for the elderly. Eventually, we will have to fit all these bridges with lifts. Second, I should have put in square red-man-green-man pedestrian lights, not round ones. Drivers sometimes mistake the round green-man pedestrian light for the green one signalling cars to go.

As for congestion charges, a few years ago, Singapore Day was held in London and the organisers put a mock ERP gantry at the entrance. I thought: "That's nice; it shows Singaporeans accept ERP as a necessary evil." During the rush hour, ERP has cut traffic volume on expressways by 15 per cent, and downtown by 16 per cent. So congestion pricing has made traffic here more manageable than, say, in Jakarta, Manila or New Delhi. But I still don't think people are convinced ERP is a good thing. Many think the government makes money from it, but it collects about $150 million a year, which is not all that much.

Kerala-born Gopinath Menon settled in Singapore in 1954. He was Singapore's chief transportation engineer from 1991 till he retired in 2001. He teaches at Nanyang Technological University and is now a freelance consultant.

I trained Singapore's first tour guides

Geraldene Lowe-Ismail, 76, started Singapore's first training
course for tour guides and trained hundreds of them

Up till the 1960s, passengers of ships that made stops at Singapore would just hire a taxi at the docks to tour the city. Half the time, the taxi driver couldn't speak English and so would just take the tourists around the Padang, up and down Mount Faber, into Tiger Balm Garden and then back to the docks.

Then, in the early 1960s, Scotsman George Thomson – who, as the Public Relation Officer of Singapore, advised the government on protocol – decided that people who wanted to be tour guides should be trained properly. I was then a travel agent at the Anglo-French Trading Company and had come to know George well as he was always asking me to take posters he had printed of Singapore with me whenever I went abroad to promote the city elsewhere.

He roped me in to help him devise the Singapore Tourist Promotion Board's 50-week Tourist Guide Training Course. Our course is still running today but is now known as the WSQ Tourist Guide Course. On Saturday afternoons, he and I would lecture about 15 to 20 trainees at a time on Singapore's history and many cultures. On Sunday mornings, we'd take them around the Padang in a mini-bus and ask them: "What's this building? What's that building?" At the end of 50 weeks, they sat an examination for their tour guide licence.

When I trained hundreds of guides from the 1960s till the mid-1980s, the first thing I'd tell them was to read *The Straits Times* for the day's happenings so that if they passed, say, Victoria Theatre with their tour groups, they'd be able to tell the tourists what show was on that day. I told the guides that their job was not just about getting tourists into Singapore, but ensuring these visitors made the most of their time here.

I was born in Perth in 1934, to Eurasian parents who had first settled down in Indonesian Borneo and, between them, had Russian, Chinese, Danish and Palestinian blood.

After years of shuttling between Singapore and Australia in ships laden with schoolchildren, vegetables and smelly sheep, at the age of 15, I accepted a job as a ticketing officer at Air India's office here. After two years, I was offered the job at Anglo-French. I was there for eight years before moving on to another travel agency. In the 1970s, I went freelance, offering heritage and farm walking tours, and have been at it ever since.

I was brought up a Christian, but converted to Islam upon marrying my husband, Ahmad, in 1968. I've lived along Orchard Road all my adult life, and it is very rich in colonial history. The area around Claymore Road was home to the Scots here, while Scotts Road was named after William Scott, Singapore's former harbourmaster and postmaster.

I've often said to the Singapore Tourism Board that it should advertise the Britishness of Singapore to Commonwealth countries, especially since Singapore, unlike other former colonies, has not destroyed its colonial buildings. However many Sentosas and Gardens by the Bay you create, there's still a basic Britishness about Singapore.

In 2014, the Singapore Tourism Board awarded Geraldene Lowe-Ismail its highest honour, the Lifetime Achievement award, for having mentored tour guides here for more than 50 years.

Photo by KUA CHEE SIONG

We kept the port lights on

Electrical engineer Goon Kok Loon, 73, remembers how disruptive workers' strikes were
in the early days. He and his colleagues did whatever it took to keep the port going

In the early days of Independence, Singapore was short of electricity and, as a junior port engineer, I was on standby 24/7 to ensure that the port continued to function amid frequent blackouts and workers' strikes. My colleagues and I often had to head back to the port at night to switch its lights on again after striking workers turned them off. We even learnt how to operate its telephone switchboards. We did what we were told because it was fantastic just to have a job then.

As gangs of port unionists dominated the waterfront in the late 1960s, the Singapore Harbour Board, later the Port of Singapore Authority (PSA), needed a way to boost its productivity. Singapore wanted to emulate the ports in London, Rotterdam and Tokyo, which were switching to a new method of hauling cargo – in steel containers either 20 or 40 feet long.

Containerisation increased port productivity tenfold because it enabled 20 men to unload 5 tonnes of cargo in a day, as opposed to the usual five days of back-breaking day-and-night manual labour. It took seven minutes for 20 men to unload one tonne of goods manually from giant sling nets; a crane boom could lift a 20-tonne container in one minute.

But this also meant that the port would have to switch completely to new cargo-transporting technologies and build many new facilities. In the 1970s, Singapore asked the World Bank for help, and the bank sent Western experts, who concluded it was highly unlikely container ships would call at Singapore within the decade.

PSA, led by its dynamic and driven chairman Howe Yoon Chong, decided to build a container terminal here anyway because container ships were already doing the transatlantic run and it was plain that this was the future. So it took a loan to do so, and got experts from the International Labour Organisation to train port workers for this new way of working.

On 23 June 1972, Singapore welcomed its first container ship, the MV *Nihon*, which belonged to a Scandinavian consortium. We'd actually been in a race with Hong Kong to containerise – and we won.

By 1982, we were handling one million containers a year, with about 50 per cent of the port containerised. By 1990, that went up to five million containers and PSA operations were fully containerised except for cargo that projected out, such as logs, or which were too gooey.

From 1970, I was part of Mr Howe's team to plan and develop the port. He was very focused and expected you to be like him. He helped transform a colonial port to meet the demands of an industrialised country. Cabinet Minister Lim Kim San succeeded him, and besides consolidating some operations that Mr Howe had introduced, also developed very good links with regional ports.

Dr Yeo Ning Hong, who took over from Mr Lim in 1994, was instrumental in expanding PSA's footprint internationally. He made me head of the port's international business division where, among other things, I acquired ports in Italy, India and Portugal and negotiated the purchase of the Belgian port of Antwerp, now the jewel in PSA's crown. We sealed the deal in 2002 for about 600 million euros.

In taking PSA global, my team and I formed joint ventures with overseas ports to develop them, the first being Dalian in China; or developed a port from scratch for a country in exchange for a lease on it and the right to make money with it; or merged with and acquired companies.

We had Singaporeans ably running the overseas ports we acquired that had traditionally been managed by Westerners. These Singaporeans had honed their skills in Singapore, where the volume of cargo handled was much larger than that at most European ports. But they still faced challenges from dealing with strong European unions and adapting to local mores.

The upcoming move of the port from Tanjong Pagar to Tuas reflects how well Singapore continues to make itself relevant to the global economy. As a city grows, its port activities become less compatible with modern-day city activities, and traffic surrounding the port affects its efficiency and productivity. The waterfront is also very valuable real estate whose value most people would try to maximise.

Electrical engineer Goon Kok Loon was the Singapore Harbour Board's first scholarship holder, at the University of Liverpool. He returned to serve it from 1965, and over 38 years, rose to be head of the Port of Singapore Authority's international business division.

One of Aziza Ali's biggest struggles in running her fine-dining restaurant was over the serving of wine, as it's non-*halal* in the Islamic faith.

People still ask, where is Aziza's?

Aziza Ali, 65, opened Singapore's first fine-dining Malay restaurant, Aziza's, on Emerald Hill. She ran the restaurant from 1979 to 1998, when she was forced by the recession to close

My mother was a fantastic cook who invited 40 or 50 people to our house at one go and cooked for them all. From a very young age I was helping her in the kitchen, starting by plucking the tails off bean sprouts. She was refined in her preparation and presentation and I learnt from her.

I tried my hand at a couple of jobs, but felt none was for me. I still loved food and decided at 24 or 25 to start a food business. At that time, when people thought about Malay food, they thought of some back-alley *nasi padang* stall. I wanted to change that, so I decided to set up a Malay restaurant where people of other nationalities could enjoy my food in a nice, classy, comfortable environment.

I felt strongly that Malay food should be served in a home, and I wanted my restaurant to have that feeling. In 1978, I went to Emerald Hill and saw a vacant unit. I asked around and found out it belonged to a Mr Tong. I didn't know I could get his details from the Singapore Land Authority. Instead, I looked at the Yellow Pages and called around 80 Tongs. Finally, I got hold of the right Tong and went to his office. He thought I was mad because I offered a ridiculously low price – $50,000. That was what I could afford! He offered it to me at $250,000 and two hours later we settled at $155,000.

I helped design the restaurant with the interior designer – I didn't want busy colours, just earth tones like brown, beige and gold.

At the start, I did everything myself. Being a restaurateur, you have to know how much everything costs so that nobody can cheat you. For years I went to a wholesale market in Beach Road at 5 every morning and was familiar with all my suppliers. When that closed, I started going to Pasir Panjang Wholesale Market.

One of my biggest struggles was over serving wine. When my father found out, he didn't speak to me for a year. I know it's wrong to make something non-*halal halal.* But my thinking was that I was serving wine only to the non-Muslims, good wine that went well with my food. But I felt a huge burden of guilt spiritually. Once every three months, I would bus old men from a mosque to my restaurant to pray and eat, and give them food to take home, just to ease my guilt. And every Friday I'd send my staff to put money in the nearby mosque.

I didn't have a lot of money to advertise, but I did this: Every night, we would give a beautiful basket of hard-boiled eggs wrapped in gold foil and decorated with orchids to all the women dining at the restaurant. That was our signature. Many of our customers were from the hotels nearby, and they would bring this basket back to their hotel. Ten pairs of eyes would see it, some would ask about it, and some would then go to Aziza's.

At that time, I did not have much competition when it came to Malay food in a classy joint. We had dignitaries and celebrities from all over the world, like Chow Yun Fat and Dionne Warwick. But a year after we opened, that part of Emerald Hill I was in was rezoned for residential instead of commercial use. The Urban Redevelopment Authority took me to court. I won two cases on technicalities and lost the last one in 1995. I relocated to Albert Court, which was what I could afford, but my customers who came from five-star hotels didn't like the look of it.

Then came the recession. That affected my business, so I closed, and went to perform the Haj, which was very important to me. Since then I've done food consulting, written books, and worked on my paintings. I've had 39 offers to reopen Aziza's, but I haven't taken up any. The person who lives in my old place in Emerald Hill tells me that there are still people who knock on the door to ask: "Where is Aziza's restaurant?"

Made in Singapore: Asia's first test-tube baby

Despite his unusual beginnings, Samuel Lee, 32, says he's just
an average Singaporean who was raised like anyone else

Photo from
THE STRAITS TIMES

My friends used to tease me when we were children: "You're man-made!" I would laugh it off, but when I think about it, they're right.

I was the first test-tube baby to be born in Asia, on 19 May 1983. My father was 21 and my mother 19 when they married in 1976. They tried to conceive with no luck, until 1982 when they took part in a clinical trial under Prof SS Ratnam and Prof Ng Soon Chye. Although doctors implanted embryos into eight women, I was the only success.

I was born to great media attention, which made my parents uncomfortable. We were ordinary Singaporeans living in a three-room flat in Woodlands. My father was a security supervisor and my mother a secretary. Thankfully, the in-vitro fertilisation (IVF) was subsidised, and thus affordable to them.

My birth may have been considered extraordinary, but I was raised like any ordinary Singaporean. I played with my cousins, who were around my age, and was punished when I misbehaved. I didn't have many toys, either – it took months of pestering my father before he bought me a remote-controlled car when I was five or six.

I got my first inkling that I was somehow different from other kids when I heard other people referring to me as a test-tube baby when I was four or five. I asked my parents about it and they just gave me a simple explanation of how I came about.

I used to ask my parents for a sibling. They'd laugh and tell me it was a very difficult request to fulfil. It was only when I was older – around 13 – that I understood why and realised what my birth really meant.

But I don't think there is anything special about being a test-tube baby. In fact, when I was growing up, it didn't seem unusual to me at all. KK Women's and Children's Hospital would often organise gatherings for IVF babies and there seemed to be so many of us! Anyway, like any other baby, I, too, was born of my mother's womb.

My life has been quite ordinary, too. I attended Qihua Primary School, Woodlands Secondary School, ITE Tampines and Temasek Polytechnic before serving my National Service with the Singapore Civil Defence Force. Then I worked in sales and business development before settling on my current job as an online media consultant.

Like most Singaporeans, I love food. My hobby is travelling around Singapore trying new food with my friends. To me, Kam Jia Zhuang Seafood in Ang Mo Kio has the best chilli crab, and Ban Leong Wah Hoe Seafood at Casuarina Road has the best fish head curry.

My birthday is not a big deal in my family. I usually have a simple dinner with my parents at a coffeeshop or a mid-priced restaurant.

Prof Ratnam gave me the name Samuel. I don't know why. We did not really stay in touch after my birth. But I do email and text Prof Ng occasionally. Without them, there wouldn't be me.

You could call me an advocate of IVF. I often encourage my friends who are trying to conceive, to go for it. I love kids and would definitely want my own. But first, I have to find myself a girlfriend.

Samuel Lee, with a projection of the newspaper article celebrating his birth. A clinical trial under Prof SS Ratnam (on facing page with baby Samuel and his mother) and Prof Ng Soon Chye led to the successful birth of Asia's first test-tube baby in 1983.

How can those who have only built bus stops build an airport?

Civil engineer Liew Mun Leong, 68, talks about overcoming the scepticism and challenges of building Changi Airport to the highest quality, on time and on a limited budget

One day in 1974, Prime Minister Lee Kuan Yew flew over Boston-Logan, an American coastal airport, and when he returned to Singapore, he proposed that Singapore build its fourth civilian airport – at Changi. By then, the government had spent $800 million expanding Paya Lebar Airport. But Mr Lee thought Changi a better location because there were fewer people to resettle and one could build out to sea easily.

As we had only six years to complete the airport, we were building it even as we were designing it, instead of waiting for the design to be completed. The government had a limited budget for the project, so we had to manage costs carefully. For example, separation of the two runways should ideally be 2km, not its present 1.6km. My team also could not convince transport planners to build a direct express train line from Changi to downtown; they said there was no need for that because Singapore was so small.

My best memory of Changi Airport is also my worst. My Public Works Department (PWD) colleagues and I attended Parliament sittings twice, when MPs discussed the feasibility of building an airport in Changi. We listened to them say things like "these PWD fellows have only built bus stops, bridges and schools. How can they build an airport?" My heart sank.

The other challenge was that, to have enough land for it, the Port of Singapore Authority (PSA) would have to reclaim an area of 870ha within six years. Many in Parliament were sceptical that PSA could achieve that, so Mr Lee asked for a feasibility report.

Howe Yoon Chong of PSA, who led the study, convinced the Cabinet that PSA could reclaim the land in time. When the Cabinet approved the $1.5 billion project, then the largest in Singapore history, I was so elated.

I'd wanted to be an architect, but studied engineering instead to make my father happy. He was a fitter and his supervisors were engineers. Home was one room in Jalan Besar and, every Sunday, my job was to kill the bugs in the joints of our collapsible beds with boiling water. To my father, my ultimate achievement would be "to work under a fan" by, say, being a clerk.

So he never quite grasped the magnitude of my task in helping to build Changi Airport which, today, sits on 1,003ha of land, 66 per cent of which was reclaimed. At one point, we reclaimed land to a level lower than was needed and it would cost $40 million to top the land up with more sand. We went to Sim Kee Boon, who oversaw the project, and thought he would whack us. But he said: "It's a professional error. If you need $40 million more, so be it. But if you cheat the government of $1, I will go after you."

I was so careful about corruption that I got my colleague, engineer Patricia Chia, to check every single lunchbox which the government got our contractors to buy for us daily, at $1.50 a box. Our worksite was far from the main road but the Corrupt Practices Investigation Bureau would not allow us to ride with our contractors to Changi Point for lunch in case they took that opportunity to bribe us. But the contractors could just as easily have loaded our lunchboxes with lobster and shark's fin, so Pat had to check the boxes every day.

A good airport has the efficiency of a factory and the comfort of a hotel. So, for example, we have wall-to-wall carpeting, which costs more but reduces noise from, say, the click-clack of women's high heels on bare floors.

Changi Airport welcomed 8.1 million passengers when it opened in 1981; in 2013, it welcomed 53.7 million. We now look forward to opening Terminal 5, which may have underground connecting tunnels, as well as converting the Terminal 1 open carpark into the mega-mall Jewel.

In April 2013, United States president Barack Obama lamented to his lawmakers that, through neglect, no American airport was among the world's top 25. I thought: "Years ago, I learnt from your airports and transportation engineering dons. Now you are saying this?"

Liew Mun Leong is widely known as founding president and chief executive officer of real estate company CapitaLand. But he actually spent most of his career building Singapore airports, and is now chairman of Changi Airport Group. He is seen here with some of his airport colleagues.

We make the airport No. 1

A formidable army of people help make Changi the efficient, award-winning airport that it is. We showcase some of them here

Mohamed Roszi Rahmat, 45, baggage handling supervisor

He makes sure that his 100-strong team of luggage unloaders put the first passenger bag on the arrival belt within 12 minutes, thus helping his employer, ground handling agent dnata, achieve that Changi Airport unloading standard 99.45 per cent of the time

I've only ever worked at Changi Airport, and started as a baggage handler. When I first heard the 12-minute target, I thought: Can we make it? Most people take 15 minutes for breakfast! And in those days, we had to write down passengers' details on baggage tags while today, we have computerised scanners that beep if we send a bag in the wrong direction.

Once a pilot shuts down a parked airplane's engines, the flight-in-charge officer at the plane must send off the first container of luggage soonest to my teammates, who then put the first bag from First Class onto the belt. It's all about coordination and, usually, we have bags waiting for passengers, which impresses them and keeps Changi Airport No. 1. I remind my teammates to work with their leg, not back, muscles but most of them have back problems because once the bags come in, they think of the 12 minutes, not of themselves.

Tan Beng Luan, 60, duty manager at the airport Lost & Found counter

This former airport police constable has won five top service awards – including Changi Airport's Service Personality of the Year 2014 – for not only helping disabled passengers and tracking down lost luggage, but also opening her home to stranded passengers in the past 34 years

I joined Changi Airport's auxiliary police force in 1981, the year it opened. That same year, I took home an Italian family of four. Their lira wasn't recognised here then and they didn't have credit cards, so they could not check into a hotel.

My husband and two sons have got so used to my hosting passengers at our Woodlands HDB flat over the years that all they ask is: "Which nationality is it this time?" Our most recent guests were a Polish air stewardess, her mother and her sister in 2013. They had flown in from Manchester but could not get seats to Manila, so they spent three days and two nights with me. It was no big deal, just three extra pairs of chopsticks. They'd also run out of money to fly home but, luckily, I'd just got my $5,000 year-end bonus then, so I spent it all on buying them tickets to go home. Although I hadn't expected it, my employer SATS (Singapore Airport Terminal Services) later reimbursed me in full for it.

Photo by
STEPHANIE YEOW

Jamal Juki, 55, manager, civil engineering, civil engineering and specialised systems

He began managing facilities at the airport 20 days after it opened on 1 July 1981, in the days when one cleaner was assigned to every toilet cubicle. He now oversees the cleaning and repairing of the tarmac

It takes only an object the size of a 20-cent coin to cause an airplane disaster. Just one nut or bolt on the tarmac can puncture a plane's tyre, or fly into its engine and shut it down.

We close Runway 1 from 1.45am to 3.30am and Runway 2 from 3.30am to 5am daily for cleaning and checks. All flights are directed to the runway not being cleaned. We use huge machines to sweep and scrub the tarmac and repaint all markings, as the tyres of the very first aircraft of the day would have blackened these. Six times a month, on Tuesdays, Thursdays and Saturdays, we close the runways for six hours at a stretch, to patch the surfaces and remove the rubber deposits left by plane tyres. We used to remove these with water pressure but now use a purpose-built machine.

My maintenance challenges now come from our runways being grooved, as grooves trap dirt, and our upcoming Runway 3, which is further away and more sprawling than our present ones.

Kandasamy Elavarasu, 54, assistant residential manager

He oversees the cleaning of all surfaces at Terminal 3, including its boarding lounges, toilets and angled glass roof, by his 100-strong team from Changi Airport cleaning contractor Campaign Complete Solutions

I'd supervised the cleaning of malls and condominiums for more than 10 years before I was posted to Changi Airport in 2006. At first, I found Terminal 3 daunting because it was huge compared to Terminals 1 and 2, but I got used to it after three months.

Most of the terminal floors are carpeted to reduce noise and give an air of luxury, but they are a real challenge to clean. They are stained all the time and we have a very short time in which to dry them after cleaning them, with people milling about all the time. But cleaning the boarding lounges is our biggest challenge by far because we have only about one hour to clean all of them every day, as they are rarely empty. That is the case even when we have to disinfect them for, say, the Mers virus.

Also, from the day the airport opened, clean toilets have been our No. 1 priority, and our complaint response system is such that any passenger who complains about, say, puddles around the washbasins can see my colleagues rectifying that before he's left the toilet.

Ashraf Ali Sultan Abdul Kader, 49, manager, horticulture, airport operations

He maintains the airport's seven gardens, including its butterfly, orchid and sunflower ones. In particular, he selected the 30,000 plants for Terminal 3's 4,500 sq m green wall, a showcase of indoor landscaping

I joined the airport in 1989. I'd wanted to work here because it then had Singapore's largest and most modern nursery, at 17ha. The nursery is now on 3ha at Changi East because the airport needed land to expand.

But I'm proud to say that my team of 11 have mastered the art of enabling plants to thrive indoors. From 2007, we grew 12m-high Bornean mast trees in T3, which ordinarily shoot up to 40m in the wild. We've achieved this with skylights, an automated watering system that controls how much and how regularly plants get water and nutrients, and LED growth lights, which have certain wavelengths absent from normal light. These wavelengths spur flowers to retain their colours.

My biggest challenge is continuing to delight people with plants. I never thought I'd see the Flower Dome and Cloud Forest at Gardens by the Bay in my lifetime, but now I hope to work on Project Jewel, which will be a shopping mall within a 22,000 sq m garden the size of the Flower Dome and Cloud Forest combined.

What makes us Singaporean

You can tell a Singaporean by the way he speaks,
dresses and a whole lot of other things,
according to *Straits Times* cartoonist Adam Lee

1975 — 1984

1975

- **Manufacturing surpasses** trade as Singapore's biggest economic engine, amid a global recession from rising inflation and unemployment

- On 11 May, the last of Singapore's 915 **Vietnamese boat people** leave St John's Island for the Philippines. They had arrived here from their war-torn country in January, and Singapore's policy is to send them elsewhere with provisions for their journey

- On 2 June, Singapore becomes the first country in the world to tax rush-hour car use with the **Area Licensing Scheme** which, in 1998, is replaced by Electronic Road Pricing

- From December, those who traffic in controlled drugs face the **mandatory death penalty**

1976

- On 23 and 24 February in Bali, Singapore and the four other founding members of Asean agree at the **first Asean Summit** to work together for regional peace and prosperity

- In May, Prime Minister Lee Kuan Yew makes his **maiden trip to China** but it is only after China resumes ties with Indonesia in August 1990 that Singapore formalises ties with China

- In early June, the United Nations lauds **Toa Payoh**, the first town built entirely by Singaporeans, as a model for the world at its inaugural Habitat meet in Canada

1977

- On April 1, the authorities here launch **Operation Ferret**, rounding up more than 5,100 drug addicts by November

- In a nail-biting **Malaysia Cup final** in Kuala Lumpur on 28 May, striker Quah Kim Song scores the first goal and also the winning one in extra time for Singapore to beat Penang 3-2

- At 11.30am on 13 June, Communications Minister Ong Teng Cheong flags off Singapore Bus Service's Service 86, **the first double-decker bus here**, from Tampines Way to Shenton Way

1978

- On 3 September, Orchard Road's perennially popular **Glutton's Square** closes, with its 80 hawkers dispersed to Newton Circus Hawker Centre and Cuppage Food Centre

- Seventy-six people are killed and 69 injured in Singapore's worst industrial accident, when the Greek ship **Spyros** explodes at Jurong Shipyard on 12 October

- Six people drowned and more than 2,000 pigs die in **massive flash floods** in December

1979

- In January, **streaming in primary schools starts**, with students sitting an examination in Primary 4 to determine if they are better suited to academic or vocational pursuits

- On 24 January, the **Singapore Symphony Orchestra** has its first concert at the Singapore Conference Hall, playing as its first song, *Majulah Singapura*

- Prime Minister Lee Kuan Yew launches the **National Courtesy Campaign** on 1 June to nudge everyone here to be more considerate

- On 20 October, **McDonald's** opens its first outlet here at Liat Towers, selling a total of 40,000 hamburgers that day, a world record broken only on 23 April 1992 in Beijing

Life in Singapore changes for good, as *kampungs*
and farms make way for factories and flats

1980

- The new year sees people using the **first ATM machines rolled out by a local bank.** The Post Office Savings Bank's machines are known as Cash-On-Line tellers

- On 1 February, the partially privatised media conglomerate **Singapore Broadcasting Corporation** replaces the government-owned Radio and Television Singapore

Photo from National University of Singapore

- On 8 August, the 18-year-old University of Singapore and the 24-year-old Nanyang University merge to form the **National University of Singapore**

1981

- On 15 April, the hybrid orchid ***Vanda* Miss Joaquim** is named the national flower at Singapore's inaugural National Flower Week

- **CV Devan Nair** is sworn in on 23 October as Singapore's third president after President Benjamin Sheares' death on 12 May

- **Changi Airport** opens on 1 July as the nation's fourth civilian airport, welcoming its first flight, SQ101 from Kuala Lumpur to Singapore, at 7am

- On 31 October, JB Jeyaretnam becomes independent Singapore's **first opposition MP** when he defeats Pang Kim Hin and Harbans Singh in the Anson by-election

1982

- On 1 January, Singapore puts the clock **30 minutes ahead**, or eight hours ahead of GMT

- On 2 January, Singapore goes **metric**, replacing pound and mile with kilogram and kilometre

- In August, swimmer **Ang Peng Siong**, 21, is the world's fastest person in the 50m freestyle when he clocks 22.69 seconds at the United States Swimming Championships

- Singapore ends the year as the **world's busiest port** by shipping tonnage

- On 6 November, the **National Civil Defence Plan** is launched to help residents here prepare themselves for wars and other disasters

1983

- Seven people are killed when their **cable cars** plunge into the sea on 29 January, after the derrick of the drillship *Eniwetok* is entangled in the cableway; Colonel Lee Hsien Loong leads an eight-hour night rescue of 13 others stranded in mid-air

- On 19 May, **Singapore's first test-tube baby** Samuel Lee is delivered by Prof SS Ratnam, five years after Britain's Louise Brown is born as the world's first such baby

- On 1 July, footballer **Fandi Ahmad** is the first Singaporean to sign to an international club, Holland's FC Groningen, after a year-long stint with Indonesia's Niac Mitra

- The **Community Chest** is established to raise funds for the many charities here, with Singapore's Father of Charity Ee Peng Liang as its first president

1984

- On 20 January, the government announces that the **National Theatre**, built in 1963 to commemorate self-government, will be demolished because it is structurally unsound

- On 2 April, **Total Defence** is launched to better engage everyone here to help keep Singapore safe

- On 22 December, Chiam See Tong defeats Mah Bow Tan in Potong Pasir, and holds the ward for 27 years, making him Singapore's **longest-serving opposition MP**

- Also on 22 December, Singapore has its **first women MPs since 1970** when Yu-Foo Yee Shoon, Dixie Tan and Aline Wong win in the general election

A NATION FORGES AHEAD

The public transport system gets a much-needed boost with the launching of the MRT system. Here the first trains arrive at a container terminal in May 1986.

Photo by SIMON KER

Singapore Girl, you're a great way to fly

You may have seen Lim Suet Kwee's wax figure in London's Madame Tussaud's wax museum in the 1990s. The 50-year-old was also the face of SIA in the 1980s and 1990s, appearing in print and broadcast ads

Photo from LIM SUET KWEE

In 1992, I was six years into my job as a stewardess for Singapore Airlines when I got a call from the management: "You're going to Madame Tussaud's in London." I assumed it was for a promotional visit to our offices there, and thought: "Wow, a free visit to Madame Tussaud's." At the museum, a lot of people looked very closely at my face. I was thinking: "This is a very weird assignment." Then the general manager said: "Congrats! You've been chosen to be the face of Singapore Airlines as a waxwork in our museum." I laughed and said: "Sure." Then she said: "I'm serious." They got to work straight away, taking detailed measurements and thousands of photographs of me, from every single angle. They had swatches of hair and skin colours they would hold up to my face to see which matched most closely. They took a mould of my hands, feet and teeth. It took the whole day and I flew to London for five more sittings after that.

Even my husband didn't know about the wax figure – we had to keep it a secret until it was unveiled. For the official launch, I told my husband we were going to London for a holiday. When we were at the museum and I saw it for the first time, it gave me goosebumps. The museum had done a great job.

I did a few commercials in the 1980s and 1990s. The most memorable was called Around the World. We went literally around the world for that – to South Africa, Greece, New Zealand, China, the United States and England, over six weeks, all for that one commercial. We went to locations where no one would normally travel to, where SIA didn't even fly to. In New Zealand, I was flown by helicopter to the top of a high cliff. I was there on that cliff by myself, taking instructions through a walkie-talkie from the director in the helicopter. He would say things like, move forward, move forward, but I had no idea where I was walking; I just tried really hard to look cool. We also did a shoot on the plains of a private game park in South Africa. I had to twirl around while a herd of zebras grazed behind me and vultures circled overhead. I was quite nervous and kept asking the director: "How long more do you want me to do this?"

When I joined SIA in 1986, I did two years on the regional fleet before I went on to the 747. The 747 was something we all looked forward to, because it was more prestigious, and took us to further destinations. My two favourite destinations were San Francisco and London. In those days, long-haul flights like those to Los Angeles and back – via Taipei and Honolulu – could take up to 16 days. We would get to spend around three days at the destination.

One flight that has stuck in my mind is the Golden Caviar service we did on a flight to London. We introduced golden caviar in First Class, and served it with Krug champagne. We had ice carvings of the SIA logo on our trolleys, which we rolled out with the cabin lights dimmed and with dry ice effects. It was so beautiful.

My final flight was also the last flight of the 747, and it also marked the 25th anniversary of my flying career. It got a bit emotional. I met many customers I knew. At one point, I was in First Class and was told a passenger in Economy needed to speak to me. I was the in-flight supervisor, so I thought something had gone wrong. But it turned out to be two guys in their 20s, and one jumped out of his seat and said: "Ms Lim, I grew up watching your commercials!"

Lim Suet Kwee has been called the face of SIA. She was the model for a Madame Tussaud's wax figure, the first Singaporean to have her likeness recreated in the famed museum, and also fronted several commercials for the airline.

He started out as a furniture painter and Lim Pok Chin is now the multimillionaire owner of Scanteak, ranked as one of Asia's best businesses.

I wanted to be the Ikea of Singapore

Lim Pok Chin, 62, owner of household name Scanteak, went bust twice in the furniture business but he now owns 100 stores in Taiwan

In 2012, *Forbes Asia* magazine named Scanteak, my furniture company, as one of Asia's best businesses under $1 billion. I never imagined that I would receive such an award.

My father died when I was a year old, so my mother raised me and my three siblings by fetching water, chopping wood and washing clothes for households here. In 1969, when I was 15, I went to shops along Victoria Street, hoping to be taken on as a carpenter. I was hired as a furniture painter instead, for $40 a month. I soon earned enough to buy my mother a small radio. She would hold it between her ear and mine so that we could listen to it together.

Within five years, I could not only paint, but also design, sell and deliver furniture. One of my boss's suppliers gave me half of the $20,000 seed money I needed to set up my own business; the rest came from my savings. So, in 1974, I set up shop at 155 Joo Chiat Road and named my furniture business Hawaii Interior Decoration, after the TV show *Hawaii Five-O*. People remembered the name of my business easily without my having to pay to advertise it.

I used to mark up my items for sale for less than the industry average of 30 per cent. That gave me such low returns that, by 1978, I was almost bankrupt. Fortunately, a former girlfriend and my elder sister gave me the money I needed to re-engineer my business. After that, I grew it even more. My dream was to be the

Ikea of Singapore. I was the first Singaporean to open a furniture shop in a mall, in Beach Road. I also opened a 24,000 sq ft showroom at Marine Parade. My competitors called me crazy for doing so.

Then the owner of France's Fly Furniture saw how big my business was, and let me franchise his business in 1984. Unfortunately, the Singapore dollar soon depreciated terribly against the franc, there was no demand here for Fly's products and their pinewood furniture warped and cracked because Singapore was so humid. I had to throw everything away.

By 1987, I'd run up business debts of a few million dollars. It took me seven years to settle them. Creditors called me every day and whenever the phone rang, I shivered more violently than someone with Parkinson's Disease. They eventually let us pay them back in instalments, and my wife Catherine and I sold off our four properties, including our Kembangan home – all at a loss – and bought a much smaller house to live in. My wife cut down on tuition classes for my three children, the whole family took buses instead of taxis to get around town, and we went to Cameron Highlands, Fraser's Hill and Port Dickson for breaks instead of to China, Japan and Hawaii, where we'd gone in better times. Our idea of a party was a barbecue at East Coast Parkway.

We did not celebrate being out of debt; there are many ups and downs in life, so one never knows what is around the corner. But I appreciated life much more after 1994, and contributed more money to those in need.

I built my business up again slowly, by focusing on building my brand, being more alert to risks, opening boutique stores instead of massive showrooms like before – and setting aside 10 per cent of my profits as reserves. Money makes one more confident.

I opened my first store in Taiwan in 1996. I now have a chain of 100 stores across Taiwan, with capital of about $200 million. In 2010, when I listed Scanteak there, its share price was 50 Singapore cents; it's now about $5.

In 2008, despite the global financial crisis, I entered the Japanese market because the Japanese like furniture made from solid wood. We now have a total of 11 stores there, overseen by my son Julian.

To succeed in life, your heart must be clear and clean, and you must not take shortcuts. I tell my children: "Be humble. All that we have today was given to us by our employees, our customers and our suppliers."

I want to do more for the elderly

Dr Kanwaljit Soin, 73, is a champion of several national issues – in particular, women's rights and support for the elderly – and was Singapore's first female Nominated Member of Parliament

When the papers reported in 1992 that the government was looking for a new batch of NMPs, many people were very excited. I was president of Aware at that time, so I rang up a few women and said: "Please apply." They all said no. I then decided I had no moral right to persuade them to do something I wasn't doing myself. So I applied, even though I had no idea what a parliamentarian did.

I've heard that I apparently hold the record for the most questions asked in Parliament. When I met civil servants, they would tell me: "Do you know, every time you ask a question, it costs the civil service money? We have to do research to answer it." But that meant I got a lot of statistics from the government, because it had to reply to me. If there's one thing Parliament taught me, it's that if you want to be in any area of policymaking, it's important to get the statistics right. If the statistics are wrong, you get shot down and the rest of what you're trying to say gets lost.

But as the first woman NMP, there was a lot of pressure to "represent the whole sex". Men don't have that pressure – for men, if you're an NMP, you just try to be a good NMP. But if a woman didn't do well, people might say: "What's the point of having a woman then? She didn't make any difference anyway." You feel the weight of not wanting to let women down, because you don't want people to be less disposed towards having women at the next NMP selection. You have to work harder to prove yourself, but it makes you stronger and better prepared for the next challenge – so it's not all bad. Subsequently though, you must make sure to encourage other women. Someone has to start, and once you've done it, you have to make sure there's a pipeline, because otherwise it's wasted. Once you've opened the door a little, you must open it wider!

What I really consider my biggest achievement was moving the Family Violence Bill in 1995. Even though it was defeated then, many of its provisions ware subsequently incorporated into the Women's Charter. So it was deferred gratification!

Two things I suggested in Parliament have now become a reality: one was that I wanted an educational (Edusave) account set up for every adult Singaporean, and the second was that I wanted a medical savings account set up for every elderly Singaporean. So 20 years down the line, both my dreams have been fulfilled by the SkillsFuture credit and the Pioneer Generation Package. Of course mine weren't spelt out as clearly as these, but these were two things I did suggest.

When you look at society in general, business, government and civil society are the three legs of the stool, but it's only recently that policymakers in Singapore have realised that it's prudent to include civil society in decision-making. If the stakeholders are just business and government, they sometimes don't see the point of view of the rest of society, especially the disadvantaged. There are a lot of Singaporeans who haven't done as well as the country's indicators seem to suggest. They still need people to advocate for them, bring out their difficulties, and try to make it so more people get a share of the pie.

I feel in particular for the elderly. They are poorer in general, and things like the Silver Support Scheme and the Pioneer Generation Package are just the beginning. We can still do better – we need to give them some autonomy and dignity. When the elderly get subsidies when they go to the doctor, for instance, their children are really the ones who benefit, because they were probably paying previously. So when you look after the elderly, the relationship in the family gets better because the children then don't feel the burden so much.

We retire way too early in Singapore. Even when I was in Parliament, we were talking about moving it up to 67. Why hasn't it changed yet? Why is there even a retirement age at all? Now, companies can retire you when you're 62 and hire you back on a contract till you're 65 at half your pay, just because there's a retirement age. If people do start to feel tired in their 60s, they should be allowed to work part-time, or take a sabbatical when they can use some of their SkillsFuture credit to learn something new. Older people have institutional memory, they have built networks, and they are loyal to organisations. People should be allowed to work for as long as they think they can, and as long as their employer finds them producing good work.

I started Wings because an academic paper commissioned by Aware and the Tsao Foundation in 2000 found that many women over the age of 40 were not well-educated, didn't have much savings or CPF, and would outlive their husbands. I started thinking, what is going to happen to these women in their old age? Someone has to look out for them, and point out their plight to policymakers. Some people asked me if I was sure I wanted to start something in my 60s, and that there'd be a lot of fund-raising and work to do. But I decided this was an issue that definitely required looking into. We were not looking at the women who were really very poor or ill – there were other welfare organisations that did that – but at women who were still young and healthy, so we could prepare them to age by teaching them how to look after their health, to save for retirement, and to form support groups. Six years on, we've been doing quite well and have more than 5,000 members and reached out to a few thousand more women.

Raffles Hotel's only resident historian, Leslie Danker, knows all the ins and outs of the famed hotel, even how high the hotel lobby is, down to the last millimetre.

Meet me at the Raffles

In the 1980s, the iconic Raffles Hotel was in disrepair and its future was uncertain. Leslie Danker, 76, who is its longest-serving employee with 43 years under his belt, recalls the ups and downs

As a boy, I admired Raffles Hotel's high ceiling, huge arches and carved cornices. I walked past the hotel on my way to and from my school, St Joseph's Institution. "How nice it would be to work in this hotel," I thought. But as much as I dreamt of working at the Raffles, I did not ask for a job there after leaving school because I was afraid to join what, to me, was such a different world then. I was then also committed to social work at the Sacred Heart Church here. So, for 15 years, I cared for polio victims, whom I still visit today at the Singapore Cheshire Home in Serangoon Gardens.

By 1972, I needed a change of pace desperately so, yes, the first place I walked into for another job was the Raffles. I met its general manager, Roberto Pregarz, who put me in its maintenance department, to work with plumbers, painters and electricians. I thought: "I'm going into the hospitality industry to meet people, not work at the back of the house." But I learnt what I could and by 1984, was promoted to front office supervisor.

I worked through so many weekends, spending nights at whichever suite was vacant, that my wife Theresa asked me: "Are you married to me or to the hotel?" By the 1980s, the Raffles was cracking and leaking everywhere, and there were rumours that it would be pulled down and we'd all lose our jobs. By then, many modern, computerised hotels were coming up along Orchard Road. I'd never touched a computer; what was I going to do?

Finally, on 16 June 1980, *The Straits Times* reported: "Raffles Hotel's future assured". DBS Land began restoring it only in 1989, after the hotel was gazetted as a national monument in 1987. In early 1989, the hotel's new chief executive, Richard Helfer, asked me: "I can see you have a great love for this hotel. Would you like to stay on with the new Raffles?" I said: "Thank God." But I did feel guilty signing my new employment contract, as not one among my 300 or so colleagues then was rehired.

When the hotel reopened in 1991, everything was computerised. Previously, we'd done everything manually; for example, we'd transfer each detail on a guest's registration card into separate books. The hotel had a room full of all these books, dating back to 1910. But at the age of 52, I had to learn how to type and use a computer.

I saw a real-life tiger at the Raffles in 1986, the Year of the Tiger. A van came right up to the gate near the Raffles Hotel's Bar and Billiard Room. Three handlers from the visiting Chipperfield Circus got out of the van – along with a 113kg Bengal tiger named Seta. It was not muzzled, and the men escorted it to the room where, as the story goes, a tiger was killed under one of its tables.

I was watching all this from behind a nearby pillar – along with eight policemen, each also stationed behind a pillar, with his rifle at the ready, in case the tiger attacked someone. Mr Pregarz had thought up this publicity stunt to fete the Year of the Tiger, but in the end, only he and the handlers were allowed near Seta, because the flash from onlookers' cameras might upset the tiger. In 1902, a tiger had been at the Raffles, and was shot dead by CM Phillips, the principal of Raffles Institution. But it had been killed under the raised floor of the room, not under a table, as the legend goes.

I was made the hotel's first resident historian in 2004, as most of our guests always ask about the hotel's history as well as Singapore's. So five days a week, I tell them the hotel's history for half an hour while showing them old and new photographs from my album, and then take them around the hotel. I get as many as five tour requests a day, and also do a lot of media interviews as well as advise documentary makers.

Every night before I turn in, I reread my thick black binder of hotel press releases and restoration documents. On the train to work five days a week, I reread my files of newspaper cuttings on Singapore history and, at lunchtime, I nip over to the National Library nearby to refresh my facts. A guest once asked me how high the hotel lobby was; I borrowed measuring tools from the maintenance department so I could tell him: 17.936m.

Once a teacher, always a teacher

Belinda Charles, 65, spent 39 years as an educator – with 21 of those years as principal of St Andrew's schools – before retiring in 2010. She is currently the dean of the Academy of Principals

Teaching was never in my sights. But I was quite an active student at Marymount Convent, and when my principal asked me to go back for a stint of relief teaching when I was 18, I said OK. That was how I got hooked on teaching. It was the most wonderful feeling in the world, that first time I taught something in class and saw the students understand it. It was such a sense of accomplishment. I went to the staff room after that class, and the teachers there took one look at me and said: "You liked it, didn't you?"

The first school I taught at as a full-time teacher was Tanjong Katong Secondary Technical School. When I started there in 1971, I hadn't quite turned 21. I learnt very quickly that students always test you, and you must never lose your cool. Students would try to throw chalk at me while I was writing on the board, and I would turn around and say: "Really, you should learn to throw it when I'm looking. Have some guts for goodness' sake!" That stopped the chalk-throwing.

The next school I went to was Nanyang Junior College as head of English, then to Bukit Batok Secondary as principal, and then principal at St Andrew's Junior College in 1990. I was there for 12 years, and then at St Andrew's Secondary School for nine years before I retired, making it 21 years in the St Andrew's family.

As principal of SAJC, I learnt that in junior college, students needed only one A-level pass and two O-level passes to go from JC1 to JC2. I thought: "Even with two As and two Os, you can't get into a university!" So I told the students they now needed two A-level passes and two O-level passes to go on to JC2. It was just one A-level pass more, but can you imagine the fuss when I announced this? My name was in graffiti in the toilets. My teachers were horrified. I started putting students in danger of not meeting the standards on my watch list and began meeting them as early as the first mid-year examination. These became known as the "Principal's Tea Sessions". I would see 200 or 300 students every year, meeting them one by one in my office from 7am to 7pm.

Many of the students still come back and say: "Thank goodness you did that." There was one boy that I was particularly worried about because he would go home every day and just play basketball. When it was one week before the examinations, I said: "I'm taking you home with me. And you jolly well come and study." He was shocked. I had permission from his parents of course. I turned him around eventually and he did OK. That was a long time ago, but that boy still came to my husband's funeral last year with his parents. They said they were grateful for what I had done to help their son.

I can tell you, every principal wants to teach again. You will never be a head of department or a principal if you are not a good classroom teacher. That's where your credibility comes from – the fact that you can teach. Every principal longs to go back to teaching, but sometimes it is not possible.

For me though, I've always found ways to stay in the classroom. In Bukit Batok Secondary, I put all the unmanageable students in one class, so of course I had to be one of the teachers that took that class. It was actually very helpful because then I knew what the teachers were going through. I learnt that many transactions go on at the back of the classroom, so I learnt to teach from the back door. This is something I still share with teachers. You need to walk around, and sometimes the best place to teach from is the back.

In my second year at St Andrew's Secondary, there was a bunch of Secondary 3 boys who had failed their fifth subject. They couldn't drop it because it was compulsory to take five subjects, but they told their teachers they couldn't do it. One teacher said some boys wanted to do Literature instead. Literature was in the doldrums at that time and teachers had asked me to close the programme, which I did reluctantly. Now no teacher wanted to cram two years' worth of Literature curriculum into these boys' Secondary 4 year. So I said I would do it.

This turned out to be one of the nicest classes I ever taught. St Andrew's boys are special – they are not scared of you. They would come in and we would do the lesson for an hour, and believe it or not, they would stay back one more hour looking over all the books in my study and just chatting with me. There were only 10 of them, and it was wonderful. Then word spread that this class with the principal was actually rather fun. The next year, the class got bigger! After that year though, my teachers took the class back. But the boys from that first class still keep in touch with me.

I used to make every child, both in SAJC and SAS, prepare five self-addressed envelopes, paste a stamp on each and give them to me when he graduated. At the end of every year, I would write a letter to current students and change it slightly for the former students, just to keep in contact with them after they graduated. So for five years I was still talking to them, reminding them of what's important, reminding them that they are special. Many of them come back and tell me they are always shocked each year to get mail in their own handwriting because they'd forgotten all about it, but then they open it to see my letter. And many of them say: "It really means a lot to me."

Belinda Charles at St Andrew's Secondary School, where she was principal for nine years before her retirement in 2010. She spent 21 years of her nearly four decades in education as principal within the St Andrew's family of schools.

I write the songs that make Singaporeans sing

Singer-songwriter Dick Lee, 59, of *Mad Chinaman* fame writes the folk songs of Singapore today, including the much-acclaimed National Day theme song, *Home*

I'm a seventh-generation Peranakan. I cannot speak Mandarin and I'm not Malay. My parents brought me up in a very English way so, as a child, I thought I was one of Enid Blyton's creations.

But when I went to art school in England in 1978, after completing my National Service, I got a rude shock. I was invisible to others when I walked the streets of London, even though I'd made it a point to socialise only with Britons, forming a band with a few of them and writing songs for it.

I sent these songs to music publisher Warner Chappell, which called me in for an interview. When I walked into its London office, the person who was to interview me got a shock. He'd thought Dick Lee was a white man. Then he said: "The most interesting thing about you is that you are Chinese. But why don't I get a sense of that in your music?"

He did not sign me on, but what he said certainly made me think. If I didn't know who I was, what kind of music was I making? I'd actually thought of staying on in Britain then, but I decided to return to Singapore, to look for what he said was missing in my music.

I came back and hooked up with record company WEA's Singapore chief Jimmy Wee. The first two WEA albums I made, *Life In The Lion City* and *Return To Beauty World*, flopped. But Jimmy believed in me and kept pushing my music until we realised that it just wasn't working. So I switched tack and sang pop covers.

Then in the mid-1980s, the National Day songs appeared and the National Day Parade began to take on a different look, feel and purpose – to build national pride. In 1987, playwright Michael Chiang's *Army Daze* was a hit and gave him and me the confidence that Singaporeans were ready to connect with themselves. So we wrote the musical *Beauty World* in 1988, which was another hit and, on the tails of that, I released my album *Mad Chinaman* in 1989.

That album, which had my versions of folk songs such as *Rasa Sayang* and *Mustapha*, went platinum here within two months of its release. But the Singapore Broadcasting Corporation banned my take on *Rasa Sayang* because of its Singlish lyrics. So schoolchildren and their grandparents were chanting it but the authorities here did not condone it.

I soldiered on, as *Mad Chinaman* was also a hit in Japan, and led to my music career in Asia. The music industry in China, Hong Kong and Taiwan wondered how this Singaporean had managed to break into the Japanese market.

I used to be so unsure about who I was musically because I was often put down and turned down. I'd drop off my cassettes at record companies such as Polygram every two weeks and they'd say: "Oh, it's you again." I don't know if they even listened to any of my songs. But you keep at it. And believe in yourself.

Some say I'm fortunate not to have had to work to support my parents, but remember, I became a musician only at the age of 34. Before that, I started my own fashion businesses without any of my parents' money. The opportunities I've had are available to every Singaporean; you just have to make the most of what you have and go out and do it.

So what's not to love about Singapore? It's the place that made me who I am. I'm writing its folk songs, such as my 1998 National Day theme song *Home*, and I'm so privileged to be able to do this.

When people say we lack freedom here, I say Singapore is like a young child whom you would not let loose in the street. You'd restrain him and nurture him so he can grow. He'd hate you for it, but what else would you do? Give up on him? At some point, you will have to let him go, but only when he is a little older, right? And Singapore at 50 is still so young.

In my teens, I performed a lot on television with my brothers and schoolfriends. Then, in 1973, The Quests' lead singer Vernon Cornelius got me to be a guest performer on Talentime. That meant I had to perform two songs every week on Rediffusion until the final. I performed songs I had written and, for the final, wrote a song called *Fried Rice Paradise*, peppering it with Singlish.

At that time, most people here didn't have a strong sense of being Singaporean. Not only did they still feel that the British way was the proper thing, but being colonised had also relegated our colloquialisms to street corners and back alleys. As a result, Radio Television Singapore banned *Fried Rice Paradise* because of its Singlish.

I hope more musicians here strive to make Singaporean music, in the way that theatre practitioners here are creating Singapore plays. We should hear people here going: "Wow, this is so local and so great!"

Singer-songwriter Dick Lee is the creative director for this year's National Day Parade – as he was in 2002, 2010 and 2014 – and is writing a new song for SG50. He won the Cultural Medallion in 2005.

Kenson Kwok, founding director of the Asian Civilisations Museum and the Peranakan Museum, joined the National Museum of Singapore when it alone made up the entire Singapore museum scene, and saw the sector grow strongly in the past two decades.

Hard slog building up an art collection

Kenson Kwok, 66, talks about the tough times he had starting the Asian Civilisations Museum,
and how he made the museum experience more than just seeing whalebones

When I was hired to start an Asian Civilisations museum in Singapore, we had to be wildly optimistic. There was only one museum at the time – the National Museum – and we inherited part of its collection in the mid-1990s to start our new one, but this consisted mainly of some Southeast Asian material and the beginnings of a Peranakan collection. Our new museum was set up to showcase the different Asian cultures that Singaporeans are descended from, but at that time we had very little from China and no Islamic or Indian collection to speak of at all. We had to reach out to international collectors to borrow items, to buy us some time while we built up our own collection. Being ambitious, we wanted to approach only the best collectors.

We contacted a famous collector of Chinese porcelain and paintings, as these were areas we lacked. He had really top quality stuff, but it happened that he was also being pursued by another museum – a major one in Australia. After we both pleaded, he said: "OK, I don't have much time so why don't you both come and see me at the same time?"

So we both flew over to visit this guy. For the next three days we went to his apartment every morning and he spent the whole day testing us. He would bring out parts of his collection in boxes for us to see, and tested us on our reactions. His collection was superb, but he also had things that were not as special, and he was testing us to see if we knew our stuff. This went on for three days and on the last day, we waited with bated breath for his verdict. He started by saying: "I've decided…" – very slowly, to keep us in suspense – "…not to lend to either of you."

It was disappointing to say the least, after having been examined like schoolboys for three days to finally be told we had failed. In retrospect, I find it quite funny.

Building up a collection is quite a hard slog. It's not just fun and games, or a matter of going shopping and picking things off a shelf. Most of our collection was built up using public funds, and we always had to look out for the right objects at the right price while also hoping that someone else wouldn't come along and buy them from right under our nose, which happened many times. We had some significant failures, but also some unexpected surprises.

There was a prominent philanthropist called Dr TT Tsui, who has since died, and museums all over the world were falling over themselves to get a donation from him. He was an obvious person for us to cultivate since we were setting up the ACM at the time. I met him a few times, but because he was donating to famous museums like the Victoria and Albert Museum in London, I sensed that our museum in Singapore wouldn't be that sexy to him. So I didn't pursue him. Some time later we both attended a small dinner in Paris and he turned to me and offered me the head of a very big Buddha from his collection. I was so surprised and delighted. Within a few weeks, this Buddha head arrived, and it has been on display ever since in our Southeast Asian gallery.

In the early 1990s, there was a very limited museum-going culture. Museums had a rather dusty image and the visitors were mainly schoolchildren going to see whalebones. In those days, many people would say that Singapore was a cultural desert.

When we opened the first Asian Civilisations Museum at Armenian Street, we needed something credible to fill our galleries and we took advantage of the 1997 Hong Kong handover to get many loans from Hong Kong collectors. This was really top quality stuff that created excitement among museum-goers here because these were still early days for museum development in Singapore. But I soon found out that a few people didn't quite realise the significance of what they were looking at. A journalist said: "Looks very nice, but how come you have so many replicas?" I was horrified, but looking back now I understand – the expectations of a museum in Singapore were very low. If this journalist had seen the same pieces in the Taipei Palace Museum, he would have said: "Oh, these are fantastic!" But he hadn't expected to see the real stuff in Singapore.

And when the ACM opened at Empress Place in 2003, we were eager to get people into the museum, but had no advertising budget. All our staff had to go out and get people interested in the museum. Whenever I took taxis, I always invited the cabbies to our open houses, and asked them to recommend it to their passengers. Once, when I was walking from Armenian Street to Empress Place, a Vietnamese couple stopped and asked me for directions to the Merlion. I said: "I'm going that way, come with me. And if you have time, I'll bring you to a museum that's just on the way!" We did all these little things, just to try to spread the message.

Now, we have six major museums and prestigious overseas museums are interested enough in our collections to offer to stage exhibitions. An exhibition from our Peranakan Museum called Baba Bling was shown in the Musée du quai Branly in Paris in 2011 – the first time any Singapore exhibit has been showcased in a major Western museum. To go from one museum to all this in 20 years – it's not just amazing. It's a quantum leap.

Sister Thomasina Sewell is a nun in the Catholic order known as the Franciscan Missionaries of the Divine Motherhood. In 1961, she and 36 other nuns set up Mount Alvernia Hospital here.

Photo by KUA CHEE SIONG

You can't rely solely on prayers

After two heart attacks and more than 60 years as a nurse and midwife,
Sister Thomasina Sewell, 81, still keeps patients company every day at the
Assisi Hospice and Mount Alvernia Hospital here

The Assisi Hospice used to be a convent housing nuns, but we vacated it and refurbished it as a hospice for the terminally ill in 1992. The idea of nursing terminally ill patients is to give them quality of life. The way we care for them changes from how we do so in an acute hospital. We try to make the hospice home for such patients and their families, to help them come to terms with one another.

You cannot allow the sadness to get to you, otherwise you are of no help to patients. But people shouldn't think they have to be trained before they can be with them. Your presence is important because often, their fear is loneliness and that nobody understands what they are going through. That's why every room in the hospice has a sofa, to encourage family members of patients to stay overnight.

I feel for my patients because I remember how much my mother suffered before she died at 83, of colon cancer. I used to ask the nurse: "Can you give her morphine?" And she'd say: "We can give it to her only every four hours because that's the ruling." They were afraid that patients would overdose and die.

Thankfully, palliative care has advanced since then and these days, the practice is to keep patients pain-free by giving them small, controlled doses of morphine. I remember a 16-year-old girl who came to us crying in terrible pain. We gave her a syringe with which she could dose herself with morphine and after two hours she was sitting up and laughing. Her family couldn't get over it. I find that's the best way because it gives patients much better quality of life.

It was in 1951, during the Emergency, that I decided to be a nun. My father and I boarded the train from Kuala Lumpur to Singapore; I was to join the Franciscan order. Midway through our journey, the communists derailed our train. The British soldiers among us told us to lie flat on the floor as they shot at the communists from the train windows. I thought: "Will I ever see Singapore?" We arrived safely at the convent in Moulmein Road here.

Once, while praying in the Mount Alvernia Hospital chapel, I saw this strapping man in a wheelchair who sobbed and sobbed. I put my hand on his, to let him know I felt for him. Later, I started talking to him in the hospice. He told me he was 40 years old, cycled to work daily and had never smoked or drunk alcohol. Now he had pancreatic cancer and was given three months to live.

You can't rely solely on prayer for patients like him. Life is more than prayer for them; it's about helping them deal with the here and now. He and his wife were estranged, and they had a son and daughter aged 12 and 13. Once, while I was talking to him, a friend of his came by and told him: "Oh, you're going to get better and we'll go cycling again." I was so angry because that was not reality. But I didn't say anything because it's not for me to say anyone is right or wrong. After his friend left, we talked about reality. He was not bitter at all, but worried about his children as he and his wife weren't close. I told him: "She's still a good mother." His wife turned up eventually and didn't desert him. I put my arms around her to comfort her as she was very upset.

My other unforgettable patient was a 40-year-old Eurasian man who had been an assistant manager of lift-maker Otis. He was given six months to live and he was so at peace. He said: "Sister, all my life, I never prayed for myself. I prayed for others. Now, people are helping me more than I've helped them."

I have not got used to losing a patient; how can you? Sometimes I'll be choking back tears at the service but I try to calm myself so I'll be helpful to the families. Every quarter, we invite families of patients who have died within the last three months to an interfaith prayer service in the Mount Alvernia chapel with a Muslim imam, a Catholic priest, a Buddhist monk, a Hindu priest and a Taoist monk. We say the name of each person who has died and invite their family members to light a candle. Then we give each of them a rose.

You can see 100 different birds in a day here

Bird guide Lim Kim Seng holds the record set in 2012 for the most number of species spotted here in a year – 265 species. He can recognise 350 different birds and identify their calls

I joined the Nature Society in 1975. Back then, there would be only four people – the leader, his friend, my brother and I. But nowadays, such trips can attract as many as 50 people.

Tourists like to come here for bird-watching. Singapore is a good place because although it may have less wilderness, there are four or five different habitats like grassland, forest, coastal, mangrove – and all can be reached easily within a day with little travelling. Our guides are also better-trained.

The tourists are always surprised to see so many different birds here – we can see as many as 100 species in a day, especially when the migratory birds are around. We start early in the morning, when it's still dark, to see owls in the forest. Then, when we leave the forest at sunrise, the visitors are always surprised by the transformation when we emerge into the open. I take them to places like the central catchment area, Pulau Ubin, Sungei Buloh and even Bishan Park.

The oldest tourist I have taken birding was an 82-year-old American woman. But I don't mind older visitors – I go slow, too, and tell them often: "Let's take five." Actually, I'm the one who needs to take five because I'm laden with my bag, binoculars and telescope and need to pace myself to last the day.

The authorities have done a good job at attracting birdlife, like planting the right fruit trees, making temporary parks out of unused places, and turning canals into streams with natural banks. Except that, this being Singapore, the need to be clean is always there, but too much pruning and trimming can be disruptive to birds as they may lose their nesting areas.

In Singapore, as in other cities, birds face the problem of flying into high-rise buildings, especially those with reflective glass. We are studying if having stickers on glass façades will help.

People often ask if I keep birds at home, seeing how I admire them. I don't because I prefer to see birds in the wild, flying. But I know pet birds can bring people joy too – and if they are captive-bred, that's fine. But if they have been poached, that's not fine.

There are good reasons for people to poach birds – some songbirds can bring in $10,000 to $20,000. When I come across these poachers – which can be two or three times a year – I ask them to leave or tell them I'll call the police. But even the police need more awareness of this problem. Sometimes when I call, a perplexed response will be: "Someone's catching birds? What's it got to do with me?"

I can remember the common names and Latin names of 350 species of birds. With birds, it's not just identifying the features from top to toe and learning that one species may have a white eyebrow and another a yellow eyebrow, or that some woodpecker species have four toes instead of three. But it's also their calls you need to learn to better detect them.

When I hear a bird call, I try to memorise it – sometimes identifying it as a kind of Morse code. Or I record it and then play it back. And birds have a language, too – some calls are alarm calls, some are for contact, others for mating. So it's like remembering at least three different calls for each bird, making it about 1,000 different calls I now can identify. It took me about 10 years to do this.

You really need to know your birds and this, coupled with the fact that I've been birding for longer than most other people here, helped me set the record in 2012 for the most number of species spotted in what bird-watchers call a Big Year.

The competition was intense, with the lead spotters changing positions several times. A trip to Pulau Tekong in December helped me clinch the win with 265 species spotted, beating the old record of 247. What a year!

Once a friend texted me to say there was a rare masked finfoot in Sungei Buloh. I went late and missed seeing it by five minutes. I waited and waited. I called my boss, said I was not feeling well and wouldn't be in. I waited half the day and didn't see it.

But even if I don't see anything, a day spent out with nature is a day gained, not lost.

Lim Kim Seng, 55, has been a qualified bird guide since 2002. He takes tourists and sometimes Singaporeans to different areas to spot birds and other wildlife. He also teaches a course on environmental education at Republic Polytechnic and is the author of *Birds: An Illustrated Field Guide to the Birds of Singapore* and several other books on birds.

Zaibun Siraj once took part in an Aware parody of beauty pageants, dressed in a tight corset and high heels in a portrayal of Mis-Fit. She is now a motivational speaker and trainer.

No, we don't have hairy legs

Zaibun Siraj, 68, a founding member of Aware, the Association of Women for Action and Research, talks about its beginnings and the misconceptions back then

In 1984, I joined the National University of Singapore Society (NUSS) committee, and helped to organise a forum on women's issues called Women's Choices, Women's Lives. Hedwig Anuar, Margaret Thomas, Kanwaljit Soin, Vivienne Wee and I were the speakers. At the end, someone said: "You organise conferences, but at the end of it nothing happens. Why don't you join any of the women's organisations and do something about it?"

We all just looked at each other. The women's organisations then were largely traditional, social types of organisations and we just couldn't see them fitting in with our thinking, objectives and perceptions of what women's roles should be. We told the audience that if they would like to take things forward, we could meet again.

So we started meeting, first at NUSS, and later at Dr Soin's clinic at Mt Elizabeth Hospital. Those at that first meeting at NUSS included Lena Lim, who later became the first president of Aware. We kept meeting at Dr Soin's clinic until we realised there was some ruling about more than five people constituting an illegal gathering. So we drafted a constitution and filed for registration as an association.

We thought we would be turned down, because of perceptions of the feminist movement. But at the end of 1985 we were registered as a society. We had a big opening at Cairnhill Community Centre. Each of us took charge of a subcommittee looking at a particular women's issue, like violence against women, women in science and technology or women in the media.

Many Singaporeans were very conservative. Although the feminist movement was going on in other parts of the world, it hadn't come here in a big way.

One of our best forums was after Prime Minister Lee Kuan Yew made some statements that seemed positive towards polygamy. This was in 1986, shortly after the introduction of the Graduate Mothers Scheme. This had to do with the idea that graduate women were not reproducing enough, and the population was declining. We decided to have a forum to protest against this. By golly, did a lot of people turn up! It was at Queenstown Library and the hall was packed. That night, Mr Lee put out a statement to say it wasn't quite what he had said. But irrespective, people stood up and talked.

I have to say, Mr Lee never took action against us. This is why I've always felt he has been very fair. The place must have been crawling with secret service people but no action was taken against us.

Aware was always writing letters to the government and the media. In the 1980s, schools introduced technical education for boys and home economics for girls. I wrote in asking for home economics to be introduced for boys as well. Some years later, they allowed this. Then there were the ads: of semi-naked women on cars or with household appliances, but also worse ones – I have kept one for a supermarket in the 1980s that portrayed a woman next to animals, like a goat and a cow, on all fours like an animal herself. This is what we fought against!

I had hate mail and it was really bad, obscene stuff. In the early days, when Aware was still very new, it was necessary for us to scream at the top of our voices just to be heard. A certain assertiveness, even aggressiveness, went a long way towards putting Aware in the consciousness of the relevant organisations and the public. We wanted to serve as a searing conscience, to be the voice of those less capable of articulating their needs, fears and aspirations.

Many men called me too shrill and strident, and they would come up to me and say they were forming organisations named "Beware" and "Unaware"!

One of our past presidents invited a journalist to visit our old centre in Race Course Road. This journalist came, and after meeting us, said: "I didn't know Aware women were like this! I thought they all had hair on their legs." So stereotypical!

We have a funny side to us that not a lot of people know about. One year, we organised a "Mis-Singapore Pageant", a parody of beauty contests, which conveyed the absurdities of such contests. I was Mis-Fit and wore an agonising, rib-cracking corset and precariously high heels. Other contestants were Mis-Demeanour, Mis-Led, Mis-Represented and Mis-Understood.

Some years back, there were old jokes about Gloria Steinem, the prominent American feminist, circulating in Singapore, rehashed as Zaibun Siraj jokes. I was so proud! I think if they start telling jokes about me, that's really an accomplishment.

Lau Pa Sat, which Lim Bee Huat took over in 1996 for $8 million and renovated for $4 million, is his proudest achievement. He brought in a lot more stalls and improved the ventilation, revitalising the grand old building.

From *kopi kia* to Kopitiam King

Kopitiam Investment boss Lim Bee Huat, 63, has more than 80 outlets now. It's a far cry from his early tough days as a coffee stall assistant

When I was doing my NS in 1970 and getting $89.10 a month, I was also running a stall at the Esplanade food centre, which brought me a lot more.

It was tough, doing two jobs at the same time. But I was used to it. From the time I was eight, I was already doing two things – going to school in the day and working at night as a coffee stall assistant. That job gave me $1 a night. I had to bring people coffee, wipe the tables and clean the spittoons every night.

But I stuck to it because I had to. My family was poor. Every morning my parents would leave seven five-cent coins on the table for each of my brothers, sisters and me. Even then, five cents couldn't buy you anything. So I combined my five cents with my brother's, and with 10 cents we could get a French loaf. I even ate the offerings left by people praying on the streets during the Hungry Ghosts Festival. I would wait till the people were gone and then take the *huat kueh* to eat.

When you're hungry, that's what you have to do. I had to think of survival. With school opening, I needed shoes, books, uniforms. I had to come up with solutions myself. My thinking was that working hard was a way of life. Enjoy now, suffer later. Or suffer now, enjoy later.

So I treasured every cent that I made, and didn't spend on things like cigarettes, beer or gambling. I saved enough to bid for that first Esplanade stall at $1,250. That grew to four stalls at the Esplanade.

My first coffeeshop was at Cheong Chin Nam Road in 1977. I did well enough after that to open one or two shops every year. It's the Chinese businessman disease – if you have one, you think of two; two, you think of three; and when you have five, you think of 10.

In 1989, when I wanted to bid $2.1 million for a Bishan coffeeshop, I had to get a loan, and every bank turned me down. I was depressed. The banks wanted to work out the sums – how many cups of coffee a month did I think I could sell. In the end I got my loan. Before I bid for it, I sat there almost every day, observing the crowd and travelling patterns and knew it would be a good buy.

And it was. The crowds would stay till 3 or 4 am, and I decided to make it my first 24-hour outlet.

When McDonald's opened here in 1979, I spent three days watching their business. "Good morning sir, can I help you sir." No Singapore coffeeshop will do that. And their equipment was so shiny and sparkling. I thought, it's over, we can't take them on.

But someone told me that if we were to be second-tier, I should at least be the leader.

So I went for automation to cut labour and introduced the ice-cuber in my coffeeshops in 1982. We didn't need someone to break ice blocks with an ice pick any more; the machine made ice cubes of the right size that we could just scoop out. That year, I also requested drink dispensers, which were faster and cleaner too. I also learnt to put cheaper brands of pineapple, chrysanthemum and soya bean drinks, which people don't know the price of, on the counters. With well-known brands, people know how much they cost in the supermarket and are not as willing to pay more. That's why it's very painful for me to order drinks, especially mineral water, because I know the cost.

Quality control is also important. I was very picky about choosing the best stalls for my centres. For example, for MacPherson market, I scouted the whole of Singapore to get good food in. I charged the stall owners $2,000 rent but if they stayed open for 24 hours, they paid only $1,200.

I also incentivise my staff. Anyone who works for 10 years gets a Rolex. Every year there'll be an increment.

When I first got into the coffeeshop trade, I wanted to join the association of coffeeshop owners, but they rejected me because I wasn't Hock Chew. Later, when I became successful, they invited me to join, but I said no. I said if I join you, I might one day take over the leadership!

Of course we have labour and rent problems now. But if we are running a business, we need to expect that costs will go up in time. Singapore is politically safe, sound and transparent. Everyone is thinking of progress. If you are willing to work your way, it's doable. Everything is doable, it's whether you put in the effort.

A Taste of Home

They may have left Singapore's shores, but still retain fond links by recreating dishes that remind them of home

CHICKEN RICE

I feel very proud to be able to prepare delicious Singapore dishes such as chicken rice for my Norwegian friends. They are always very impressed by how good it tastes. I use my mother's reduced chicken rice sauce to flavour the rice, and chilli sauce, which I bring back after visiting her in Singapore.

Audrey Wong Mortensen (right), 58, in Torød, Norway for the past 20 years, with her visiting Singaporean niece, Beverly Becker, 24

BAK KUT TEH

Cooking Singapore food in China is a simple way to connect to my roots because I do miss Singapore food terribly. Eating Singapore food also reminds me of home and it is a place I want to go back to some day.

Contractor Billy Lim Jak Meng, 38, in Beijing, China for the past 13 years, with his Chinese national wife, businesswoman Kay Chen Yanji, 40

LAKSA

I think of Singapore every day even after all these years away. I have always cooked Singapore food, and I love Singapore desserts, so even though my two sons aged 13 and 15 have grown up here, they think it's normal to have Singapore food regularly.

Housewife Wern Lim, 40, in Birmingham, Britain. She has lived in various parts of Britain for the past 22 years

BAK CHOR MEE

Home is just a place – but it is the first place. And that's why bak chor mee will always take first place over sushi, ramen and tempura! (Close fight with sashimi, though.)

Lawyer Tan Sze Yao, 33, in Tokyo, Japan. He has lived in Japan for the past three years

ROTI JOHN

Roti John is one of the easiest Singapore dishes to prepare because I can find all the ingredients here easily – minced meat, onions, eggs, French loaf. It's comforting to be able to cook Singapore dishes even when you are thousands of kilometres away from home. And it's always nice to share these dishes with other Singaporean families in Utah!

Homemaker Suryani Omar, 33, in Midvale, Utah, US for the past three years, seen with her husband, engineer Muhamad Nurhakim, 33

KAYA TOAST

I grew up eating my Mum's kaya so it's really the only food I know and love. I always think of my Mum and her love for food when I make it. Watching her go through all the effort of making kaya only to give most away to family and friends taught me much of what I know about cooking today – good food takes time, effort and love, and it's better shared.

Counsellor Cherie Goh, 31, in Perth, Australia for the past 11 years, with her husband, physiotherapist Timothy Ho, 31

YUSHENG

Shredding vegetables and cutting salmon sashimi while I am away from home makes me nostalgic, especially during the Spring festival. But it allows me to share this uniquely Singaporean tradition with my Doha "family". At the same time, it also helps me to connect with my home in Singapore.

Business operations manager Philomena Gan, 53, in Doha, Qatar for the past 10 years

115

The 5 C*s

(* Complain, Complain, Complain, Complain, Complain)

Is it true that Singapore is a nation of grumblers?
Straits Times cartoonist Lee Chee Chew
makes short work of this caricature

LITTERING

WEATHER

TRAIN BREAKDOWN

SERVICE

PUBLIC TRANSPORT

1985 — 1994

1985

- Singapore has its **first recession since 1965**, with unemployment at 4.1 per cent

- On 2 September, **Wee Kim Wee** is sworn in as Singapore's fourth president, after CV Devan Nair resigns on 28 March

- On 25 November, the **Association of Women for Action and Research** is formed to campaign for better opportunities for women here

- Stock market darling **Pan-Electric Industries** collapses, closing the Singapore and Malaysia bourses from 2 to 4 December, and exposing regulatory gaps

1986

- Thirty-three people are killed when the six-storey Lian Yak Building, housing **Hotel New World**, collapses on 15 March. Seventeen others survive the tragedy

- On 4 July in Australia, Dr Christopher Chen becomes the first person in history to deliver **twins from frozen human eggs**, having pioneered that freezing technique

- **Bugis Street**, famous for its street food and transvestites, is demolished by year's end to make way for a new sewer

1987

- The **CPF Minimum Sum** scheme is introduced on 1 January

- On 24 January, **the last 1,500 nightsoil buckets** here are deposited at the Lorong Halus Disposal Station in Tampines

- On 1 March, First Deputy Premier Goh Chok Tong announces the end of the Stop At Two population policy and the start of the **"Have Three Or More If You Can Afford It"** policy

- Twenty-two people are detained between 21 May and 20 June under the Internal Security Act for being in a clandestine communist network dubbed the **Marxist Conspiracy**

- On 7 November, 120,000 people here ride the **first MRT train** from Toa Payoh to Yio Chu Kang in 10 minutes

1988

- In January, **Catherine Lim** is the first Singaporean to have her book, *Or Else, The Lightning God*, studied as an examinable O-level Literature text globally

- Changi Airport is voted the **Best Airport In The World** for the first time by Britain's *Business Traveller* magazine, and wins this title for another 17 consecutive years

- On 18 May, Parliament gives the nod to **Group Representation Constituencies**, in which at least one among three MPs must be from a minority

- In August and December, Singapore holds its **first Swing Singapore street parties** in Orchard Road, drawing crowds of up to 250,000

1989

- HDB's **Ethnic Integration Policy** means that from 1 March every one of its apartment blocks must have a mix of Chinese, Malays, Indians and other races

- On 3 March, the government announces the **revision of pay for 76,000 civil servants**

- From April, drivers crossing the Causeway must have at least **half a tank of petrol** to deter them from refilling on the cheap in Johor; this is revised to three-quarters of a tank on 4 February 1991

- On 30 April, shopping lane **Change Alley** closes for good

Amid mostly galloping growth, Singapore bids old ways goodbye and embraces new challenges

1990

- From 2 April, anyone who wants to own a vehicle must bid for a **Certificate of Entitlement**; it is another scheme to ease traffic congestion here

- Wee Soo Hup, 59, undergoes the **first heart transplant** here on 6 July. He receives the heart of a 41-year-old construction worker, in an operation by a Singapore General Hospital team led by Dr Tong Ming Chuan

- On 28 November, **Goh Chok Tong** becomes Singapore's second premier, after Lee Kuan Yew steps down, having served Singapore for 31 years and 176 days

- By year's end, Singapore overtakes Hong Kong as the **world's busiest container port**

1991

- On 26 March, Commandos rescue all 123 people on board a **hijacked Singapore Airlines plane** here by overpowering the four Pakistani hijackers in 30 seconds

- On 1 July, the government introduces a movie rating system, which allows the screening of raunchy films under the Restricted (Artistic) or **R(A)** rating

- From December, rehabilitated drug addicts are made to wear **electronic tags** which track their whereabouts

1992

- From 3 January, the sale of **chewing gum is banned** here, after globs of it freeze MRT trains and cost HDB $150,000 a year in clean-ups; in 2004, this ban is partially lifted to allow the sale of smokers' gum here

- On 1 April, the new statutory board **Institute of Technical Education** takes over and refurbishes all vocational institutions here

- On 4 August, Creative Technology is **the first Singapore company to list on Nasdaq**, the world's technology bourse. On 1 August 2007, it delists itself

1993

- From January, Singaporean students between six and 16 years who do well in most schools get cash rewards via new **Edusave** accounts

- In June, Singapore hosts **the SEA Games**, and wins a record 50 golds

- On 1 September, Ong Teng Cheong becomes Singapore's **first directly elected president**, defeating former Accountant-General Chua Kim Yeow

- On 1 November, more than 1 million Singaporeans become **shareholders of SingTel** when it launches the largest share flotation in Asia

1994

- On 26 February, Singapore and China ink an inaugural deal to develop the **Suzhou Industrial Park** jointly

- On 3 March, **Michael Fay**, 18, is sentenced to four months' jail, six strokes of the cane – later reduced to four – and a $3,500 fine; he is the first American to be caned here

- From 1 April, shoppers here have to pay **Goods and Services Tax**

- The **Night Safari**, the world's first after-hours zoo, opens on 26 May

- On 24 June, the first **Great Singapore Sale** is launched to boost tourism here

- On 17 December, Singapore beats Pahang 4-0 to bring home the **Malaysia Cup** after 14 years, but exits the tournament two months later after disputes over gate takings

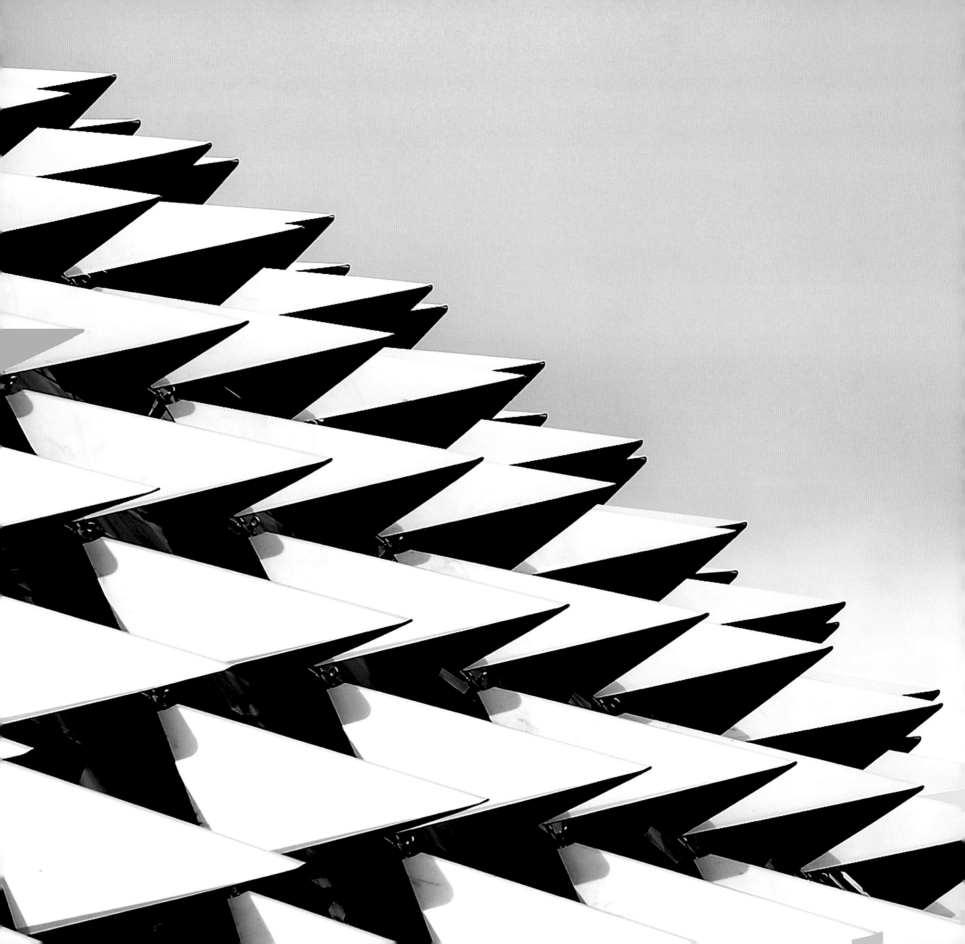

A NATION SPREADS ITS WINGS

Beyond material success,
Singaporeans want a richer,
more rounded life. The Esplanade
– Theatres on the Bay opens to
much fanfare in 2002.

Photo by JOYCE FANG

121

From watching CSI to heading a fire station

Shaiful Herman, 32, an assistant director in SCDF's HazMat Department,
was its first overseas government scholar, youngest SCDF officer to be promoted to
major and then lieutenant-colonel, and one of the youngest officers to head a fire station

I grew up geeky. I loved the TV show CSI, and I loved chemistry. I started developing an interest in forensics, so I thought maybe I should join the police. When I applied for a PSC scholarship, I listed the police as my first choice. I was called up for an interview in front of a huge panel. Nine adults asking you questions about current affairs – daunting for an 18-year-old! The head of the panel said: "I've noticed you like chemistry. Why won't you consider a career in the SCDF?"

I really didn't know much about SCDF – I thought of it as fire-fighting, saving cats maybe. That question triggered something in me, and I thought: "Why not? I can look into it." Then they arranged personalised visits for me to different departments of the Home Team, and I found my interest piqued. So when they offered me the first SCDF overseas Singapore government scholarship in 2002, I took it.

That scholarship changed my life. I had never flown on an aeroplane until I had to fly to London. All my holiday trips as a kid involved taking the MRT from Pasir Ris, where I lived, to Jurong, where my cousins lived. I had to take charge of things in my household early on because I had two younger siblings, my father was perpetually absent, and my mother could hardly speak English.

My journey was an uphill one, but I'm a determined chap, and that's an important attribute that's helped me to get where I am. Even now, I have to be careful of people thinking: "You're a scholar, things are easier for you." For example, becoming the commander of a fire station at the age of 26, first at Banyan Fire Station and then at Tampines Fire Station – people under you, they're your age, and you want to be friends, but you're their boss. And I had junior officers as old as my Dad.

So I came in with that mindset, that I had to prove myself to the people working under me. At my first posting as Rota Commander of Alexandra Fire Station, the officers had seen so many more fires than I had. But I joined them for every training session, and when any issue arose, I took charge, so they started to see that I was in control. I asked the more senior ones to share their experiences during training, and I would consult them on administrative issues. I made it a point to talk to everyone individually a few times a year, so they knew I was accessible.

Rescues are one of the best parts of my job. It's a matter of timing – just a few seconds could mean life or death. One of my most unforgettable experiences was a suicide attempt when I was just four months into the job at Alexandra Fire Station. We were called to an eighth-floor HDB flat. The window was open and police officers were already there. We peered out of the window, and saw this maid holding on to the bamboo pole holder, just hanging there. Her feet – thankfully they were small – were resting on a small ledge.

She refused to come inside. The problem was, she could speak only Bahasa Indonesia, and nobody else in my crew, and even the police, could speak Malay. So in the absence of any counsellor, I had to talk to her and try to get her back inside.

Downstairs, people were gathering and looking up. It was scary, because the last thing you want is for her to drop while you are talking to her. Everyone would want to know: "What did you say to her?" Slowly, I got her to tell me why she was doing this.

She said she wanted to jump because she had been abused. She was clinging on, but I could see she was shaking. After talking to her, straight away I offered my hand, and said: "Please, now. Just come up." And she did.

There's a reason firemen don't really wash their fire suits, says LTC Shaiful Herman. "Mine is filthy, covered in soot, but the dirtier it is, the more holes there are, the more experienced you look! You can spot a newbie a mile away by his clean suit."

I saw 2 or 3 babies die a day

As head of paediatrics at KK Women's and Children's Hospital, Dr Ho Nai Kiong, 77, witnessed
marked improvements that came with the hospital's move to its current building in 1997

When I was told to set up the first government neonatal ward in Singapore, in what was then Toa Payoh Hospital, I was a bit surprised. This was in 1977, and while there were neonatal services in other government hospitals, they were usually part of the paediatrics department. This was to be an exclusive neonatal department.

It was a terrible time – we literally started from nothing. The infant mortality rate was high, and many babies died from not being able to breathe. There were no ventilators in our ward. I would put a tube into the baby's windpipe and use a hand pump to pump air into its lungs. I had very dedicated nurses who would take over after a while, but we just couldn't pump like that for 24 hours.

Sometimes, premature babies needed warming devices, and we didn't have a radiant warmer. So we used a table lamp over the baby – completely non-scientific and no way to calculate the right dose. But we had to keep them warm somehow.

I was also the only doctor in the ward. While trying to resuscitate this baby, another baby would collapse. So I had to wash my hands and go to that one, but then another baby would suddenly decide not to breathe, and I had to rush over there.

I saw two or three babies die a day. It was only in the early 1980s that we started to see improvements. I first got one doctor, then another, to help me. We built up experience, read more, attended more conferences, and found out what people in other countries were doing. But there were other factors – we started seeing fewer sick babies born because mothers had better housing and nutrition.

I moved to KK in 1989 as head of the neonatal department, and there was a Neonatal Intensive Care Unit there. It was extremely crowded, worse than a market, and had just one ventilator. At that time though, the birth rate was also lower and we had some labour wards vacant, so I asked the medical director to let me expand into those empty wards.

Over time, the death rate came down, but it was still too high, and the biggest reason was that premature babies were dying from respiratory distress syndrome. When a baby is born, the lungs expand to take in oxygen, but for a premature baby, there isn't enough surfactant, which allows normal newborns' lungs to expand. Babies who reach 36 weeks will produce surfactant by themselves, but those born before 34 weeks don't have enough, and their lungs are very stiff. Imagine blowing air into a leather soccer ball – it can't expand.

In 1991 a big drug company asked me to take part in a multinational trial of a new drug. They gave me 100 free doses of this surfactant to try on the babies and appointed me the principal investigator of Singapore. That's how this drug, which is now so common in hospitals, first came to Singapore.

I did the trial, and we found there was an improvement. Not a 100 per cent improvement – some were very serious and we couldn't save them – but the improvements in survival rates were statistically significant. I went to the final meeting to present my results – 37 countries from all over the world attended, from South America, Europe, everywhere, but I was the only Asian guy. I felt quite proud.

When KK moved into its new building in 1997, I moved over too as chairman of paediatrics. I felt a bit sad at times because I had fought so hard for more space to improve the neonatal ICU and then had to give it all up. The new KK had a lot more space and everything was up to international standards. With more space for the babies, the infection rate also came down, and there was more equipment like ventilators as well as heart and lung monitors. There were more doctors and nurses, so more attention could be given to each newborn. We attracted a lot of visitors from overseas to come to KK to see the setup and learn what we were doing.

When I first started working in the neonatal ward, some doctors didn't believe in saving a lot of premature babies, actually. They had seen too much, and sometimes when they were trying to help them, the babies' brains got damaged. But if I thought a baby was on the road to recovery, I would try very hard. I had one baby who was 800g when born – I saved her and now she holds a senior position at OCBC Bank. The first baby with surfactant, she's now 23. So even though sometimes I feel sad that I had many babies who didn't do well, I know there were many who did. At least for some, even when I felt my hands were tied, I was able to do something to help.

Dr Ho Nai Kiong, a pioneer of the treatment of newborns, set up Singapore's first government neonatal ward in 1977. Conditions were basic and he saw two or three babies die a day, a far cry from survival rates today.

Miguel has three apples. Emilio takes away one

Singapore's Maths textbooks are translated and used around the world, and Peh Shing Woei, 39, chief executive officer of Shing Lee Publishers, wants to multiply the business

When I was in secondary school, I felt quite proud that my friends and I were studying from Maths textbooks published by my family's book company, Shing Lee Publishers. In fact, my cousins and I – there are 29 of us – are all named after the company. All the boys have "shing" in their names, while all the girls have "lee". *Shing lee* means victory in Hokkien.

This name is now familiar to students in 33 countries across the world. Between four and five million copies of our Maths textbooks are exported to countries such as Papua New Guinea, the United States, Britain, Jordan, Colombia and Mauritius annually.

It is common for American and British books to be exported. British books, because many countries in the Commonwealth take the Cambridge exam, while American books are well-received because the US has the best universities in the world. In our case, demand for our textbooks rose from global test results and research on their effectiveness. Book distributors and homeschooling parents first showed interest in our textbooks, from Primary 1 to Secondary 4, when Singapore students began placing in the top three spots in international Maths exams from the mid-1990s. Even US President Barack Obama acknowledged Singapore's effectiveness in Maths education, pointing out in 2009 how Singapore students aged 13 and 14 outperform US students three to one in Maths. Research papers by local and overseas universities like University of Washington have also referred to our textbooks and how they help students do well in Maths.

So from the late 1990s, overseas distributors have been flying in to look for our Maths textbooks. Many countries use the exact same textbooks that our students do. But increasingly, our distributors are asking us to adapt the books to local contexts. In the Philippines, for example, characters are named Emilio and Miguel, and the currency used is the Philippine peso, rather than the Singapore dollar. In the US and Britain, we are developing local editions according to their new syllabus, and in Italy, our textbooks are being translated into Italian. They have also been translated into Bahasa Indonesia.

What is unique about Singapore's approach to teaching Maths is the way we combine several methods to help students understand mathematical concepts, using real-life items, pictures and formulas. We also use a "spiral approach", meaning we teach topics according to the students' level of understanding. For instance, we may broach some aspects of algebra in Secondary 1, and revisit it with deeper concepts when the students get to Secondary 2. This is according to the syllabus set out by the Ministry of Education (MOE), which calls for tenders every few years to update its curriculum.

We rely on our team of consultants and authors, many of whom are present or past teachers with MOE, to write our textbooks. Besides problem-solving, our Maths textbooks also include real-life examples to help students see the relevance of what they are learning, as well as discussions and journal writing to develop their presentation and communication skills.

Although Shing Lee has been publishing Maths textbooks for secondary school students since 1979, and for primary school students since the early 2000s, our company had humble beginnings. My grandfather Peh Boon Poh, 99, first started a small comics bookshop on Chin Swee Road in 1935. He had arrived from Anxi County in China's Fujian province in 1929 and had been a factory worker in a wood processing plant for six years before he decided to try his hand at running a business.

Having never had a shot at a good education, my grandfather always believed that education was the only way to a better life. This was why the shop then expanded into selling educational materials, before producing its own textbooks in the 1950s. The company has since dabbled in a range of publications, from children's picture books to contract publishing, but we decided to focus on Maths textbooks as our specialty because it is a universal subject. We produce textbooks, assessment books, 10-year series for O levels and A levels, and five-year series for the Primary School Leaving Examination.

Eighty years on, we are ready to do more. Besides developing Maths textbooks for primary schools in Namibia, we are writing English textbooks for primary schools in Nigeria, and are looking into how we can also develop textbooks for Science – another subject that is common to the world. It is my hope that as more and more countries adopt the Singapore way of teaching, more students overseas will benefit, their economies will naturally improve, and they will eventually have better lives. This is what my grandfather always believed in.

Shing Lee Publishers chief executive officer Peh Shing Woei at Mainland Printers in Tuas, where an edition of the Secondary 3 Normal Academic Maths textbooks was being printed.

The art of being human

The $600 million Esplanade arts centre, nicknamed the Durian, opened in 2002. Helming it is Benson Puah, 58, who talks about why it can be a vessel to transform people

In 1998, after 20 years of building businesses in Hong Kong, Singapore and Indonesia, I got a call from Niam Chiang Meng, Permanent Secretary of the Ministry of Information, Communications and the Arts. He wanted to meet me to talk about my coming into the arts sphere here, as chief executive of the Esplanade.

I was then in the healthcare industry, and didn't even know what a permanent secretary did. I met him, mid-afternoon, at a hotel café. He was earnest and honest. I drank glass after glass of wine throughout our conversation; I wanted to show him that I was my own man, and did not have the mindset of a dutiful civil servant. The most important point he made was that the Esplanade was an important institution to help in Singapore's social transformation. I accepted that challenge because I, too, didn't see the Esplanade as just bricks and mortar or for staging shows for business, but as a vessel to transform people.

I wanted to unlock this social good that the arts can bring. Some artists think that talking about social good means compromising artistic excellence. But I think for art to do good, it must be excellent. When I started out at the Esplanade, I didn't articulate any of this publicly because the general mood then was to have as many shows by famous artistes as possible and to brag about elevating ourselves to a global city with this new arts centre.

The Esplanade then was unknown elsewhere and Singapore itself did not have a reputation among famous artistes. But those who performed at the Esplanade fell in love with it and their word of mouth was the most powerful advertising for us. While here, these artistes also enjoyed interacting with our multicultural society which we think is so troubled, but which they think is so wonderful. For example, the diversity of shows that the Esplanade offers in two months here is what other arts centres would present over five years, but because we are so multicultural, such diversity makes sense to us.

We in Singapore have to accept that we are many things. Our palates are very diverse, and our souls should mirror our palates. But while we eat three times a day, we haven't formed the habit of listening or participating in a form of expression once a month, let alone once a day.

We often like to compare ourselves to New York, London and what have you. But each city has different social dynamics and profiles. We can't aspire to be something we are not. Our own cultural evolution begins with a better understanding of ourselves, and that is an issue of identity. For example, you wouldn't mess around with our *laksa* by adding strawberries or whatnot to it.

Even as I gave the broader community here what they wanted, my team and I also forged deeper relationships, such as with volunteer welfare organisations, and introduced meaningful programmes, such as yearly cultural festivals and shows for children and the elderly.

One evening, shortly after the Esplanade opened, I was walking on its rooftop when I met a man. I started talking to him, and he lamented that the lepers he helped would never have a chance to see the Esplanade, as people would not want them around there. I said: "Why not?" and arranged for the lepers to visit.

Whenever I am stressed, I either run or play the piano, which I'd learnt from the age of five. In school, I organised drama festivals, played the clarinet and performed folk dances. All this honed my belief that any form of art is valuable as it can help anyone under pressure cope better, as well as engage with everyone else.

Art is a blunt instrument for social transformation, but if you use it to strike at the same spot consistently and persistently, it will yield eventually. Such persistence must come from a place that is sincere, authentic and not contrived. Otherwise, if you try to engineer something purposefully, it will fail because what you're trying to do would be so evident to the cynics, and you'd only appeal to the converted. Singapore is an improbably successful nation, so we focus a lot on economic well-being. But surely the definition of a person must go beyond his pay cheque? Surely our hobbies are not walking about in malls and shopping for cars and houses? So the arts is an important strand of our DNA that we should nurture.

Well-known names in the arts and entertainment circles get together for a shoot at the Esplanade Theatre

This page:

Top row *(from left)*
Najip Ali, 51, television host; Eric Khoo, 50, film director and Cultural Medallion recipient; Jack Neo, 55, film director and Cultural Medallion recipient; Ivan Heng, 52, theatre director (W!LD RICE) and Cultural Medallion recipient

Middle row *(from left)*
Anna Lim, 53, DJ from UFM 1003; Liang Wern Fook, 51, *xinyao* music pioneer and Cultural Medallion recipient; Fann Wong, 44, film and television actress; Billy Koh, 52, songwriter and music producer; Zoe Tay, 47, film and television actress

Bottom row *(from left)*
Ken Lim, 51, composer, artiste manager and music producer; Goh Lay Kuan, 76, pioneer ballet dancer and Cultural Medallion recipient; Santha Bhaskar, 76, Indian classical dancer and Cultural Medallion recipient; Ong Keng Sen, 52, theatre director (TheatreWorks) and Cultural Medallion recipient; Lim Kay Tong, 61, veteran film, television and stage actor

After 20 years in hospitality and tourism, Benson Puah set up and still helms Esplanade – Theatres on the Bay, Singapore's renowned arts centre. He also headed the National Arts Council from 2009 till 2013, during which time he had a bout with cancer, which is in remission now.

This page:

Top row *(from left):*
Gurmit Singh, 50, television host and film and television actor; Aaron Aziz, 39, film and television actor; Hossan Leong, 46, comedian and television host; Kok Heng Leun, 49, theatre director (Drama Box) and Cultural Medallion recipient

Middle row *(from left):*
Kit Chan, 43, singer and actress; Jeremy Monteiro, 55, jazz pianist and Cultural Medallion recipient; Som Said, 64, Malay classical dancer and Cultural Medallion recipient; Xiang Yun, 54, film and television actress; Brian Richmond, 68, veteran radio presenter; Ramli Sarip, 63, rock singer and songwriter; Kuik Swee Boon, 42, contemporary dancer and Cultural Medallion recipient

Bottom row *(from left):*
Joanna Wong, 76, Chinese opera performer and Cultural Medallion recipient; Tay Teow Kiat, 68, Chinese orchestra conductor and Cultural Medallion recipient; Atin Amat, 58, pioneer Malay theatre practitioner (Teater Kami) and Cultural Medallion recipient; Patrick Chng, 47, singer and local indie music pioneer

I waded into the waters of Meulaboh

Major Vincent Yeo, 39, was in the Singapore Armed Forces advance team that flew into Indonesia just after the 2004 tsunami. He still remembers the overwhelming smell of death

The flight from Medan to Banda Aceh took 45 minutes, and I spent the whole time staring at the devastated coastline – whole villages flattened, entirely wiped out. You could see only these square boxes that had been the foundations of the *kampung* houses. It was a heartbreaking sight that made me ask myself – can anyone have even survived this? The scale of destruction was just so large. I vowed to myself that I would do everything I could for the people of Meulaboh.

When the tsunami wrecked large parts of Asia on 26 December 2004, I started preparing my officers for overseas deployment. We had no idea how long we would be gone, and how much to pack – even things like the number of rice cookers and toilet rolls. I told the crew: "Don't expect this to be a short trip." But there was no issue getting people to sail. The crew all felt a moral obligation to help.

I was part of the advance party which flew into Meulaboh as part of the SAF's relief efforts, and the only naval representative. Singapore was the first foreign country to be there to offer help. When we got there, a lot of people were still in a state of shock – many were still crying, looking for their family members. It was the first time I had encountered the aftermath of such a disaster.

I had to look for a suitable site for our landing craft to bring aid from our Landing Ships Tank (LSTs) to shore. I checked the coastline, going fully into the water to check the hydrographical conditions of the shore, seeing how deep the water was and checking for underwater obstructions.

On the first day, I found that the first stretch of beach I went to – certain parts were quite deep and the surf was over my head – was not suitable because there were too many sand banks. That would cause the fast craft to ground. The last thing we wanted was another problem during the disaster relief operations.

The second day, I saw a breakwater that had been partly destroyed by the tsunami and found that it could work as a landing site, because it was naturally deep. Three of our LSTs soon arrived and we got to work, providing humanitarian aid, medical supplies and engineering vehicles to the Indonesians. Part of my job also involved making sure everyone was accounted for and back on board at the end of the day – the place could get quite dark in the evening, and there was also the constant fear of a second tsunami.

Whatever you saw in the news, it was a lot worse. The smell of death was overwhelming, especially from the bodies soaked in seawater under the hot sun. Those are the kinds of things you can't learn through TV. The Indonesians offered us masks because of the smell, but they themselves were not wearing them, so I decided not to. I wasn't there as a tourist, or to work comfortably. If the locals were not going to put them on, then I didn't see the point either.

Towards the end of the mission – we stayed for 21 days – I saw a group of children playing near a school. I gave them some sweets, and seeing them made me happy, because it meant some normalcy had returned to their lives. You really see how resilient people can be.

You get a lot of exposure over the years to different kinds of difficult situations. I was also part of the first SAF mission to the Middle East, when we were deployed to Iraq. We were there as part of the reconstruction effort. Terrorists had blown up one oil terminal, so we were to guard the remaining one. We were on close, friendly terms with another ship there, the USS *Firebolt*. Three months after we came back, the USS *Firebolt* was involved in a terrorist attack, and three of the crew died. It was very sad and our whole crew was shocked.

Like it or not, we are a maritime nation. Ultimately, all sea lines affect us. If fuel or food fails to be shipped to Singapore, we are in trouble. We cannot afford any disruptions in shipping routes anywhere, so we have to go out on these missions. And that's why I tell the recruits, even in peacetime, we can't take anything for granted.

Major Vincent Yeo, the head of the Navy Recruitment Centre, was the executive officer of RSS *Endurance* during Operation Flying Eagle, SAF's mission to Aceh. He was the only naval representative in the advance party that flew into Indonesia a few days after the 2004 tsunami struck.

Fighting Sars at Ground Zero

Dr Tai Hwei Yee, 57, took over the management of all Intensive Care Units
in Tan Tock Seng Hospital when the Sars epidemic hit Singapore in 2003.
A total of 33 people died and 238 were infected over three months

I'm not sure people can ever really understand what it was like in the hospital. The fear that we had for our own lives, for instance – it's something you can talk about but it's very hard for another person to understand. We were scared, and we were obsessive. We turned up for work every day not knowing enough about the disease or what we could do to protect ourselves, just thinking: "I hope I'm not the unlucky one today."

We all knew that the first sign of trouble was a fever, and as you went through your work, you might start to feel hot and flushed, and then you started thinking: "Oh my God, I'm feeling hot." We were all obsessively taking our temperature every couple of hours, and doctors who were sleeping at the hospital woke up every few hours just to check their temperature.

Things happened very, very rapidly. Initially, the first few patients were actually our staff. Having colleagues admitted to ICU – you can handle that. We know that ICU care is very good. But actually having a patient die on you, who's a member of your own fraternity – that's the hardest.

One of the worst moments was when one of our physicians, Dr Ong Hok Su, died in April that year. He had actually been improving. I was in our control room with a couple of operations people. Everything looked peaceful, and suddenly we got a call from the ICU to say that Dr Ong had passed away. I was stunned. I asked: "How can that happen? I thought he was getting better?" They said he had been getting better, but was still dependent on oxygen, and had walked to the toilet on his own. He collapsed, and they couldn't resuscitate him. Before that, the mood was getting better – we were getting fewer patients, we could see patients recovering because of new clinical treatments. We felt we could see the light at the end of the tunnel. Then suddenly this hit us.

It amazed me how people rose to the occasion. One example: Almost overnight, we had a lot of ICU bed requirements for our confirmed Sars patients, and all the beds on the sixth-floor ICU were filled up. I was coordinating all the ICUs during Sars, so I had to deal with it, but here's the thing: The ICUs on the sixth and third floors were designed differently. The sixth-floor medical ICU had independent air flow for every single room. But surgical ICU patients – on the third floor – had common air flow between the rooms. So we could not place Sars patients in the third-floor ICU. We had to figure out very quickly how to convert some of the other rooms to a one-way air flow system.

Our engineering people were wonderful. Within three days they got these huge industrial extraction fans, sealed up our high dependency rooms, cut holes in the windows to install these fans and created one-way air flow – essentially adding extra ICU rooms. It's a level of support you never see during peacetime, but comes out only in a crisis.

We were lucky because very early on we adopted a few measures, although at that time we weren't 100 per cent sure if they would work. It was a combination of factors – good foresight, good analysis and simple good luck – that helped us get on top of it. Somehow, we made the correct decisions about understanding the role of fever and the mode of transmission. Many people were saying that it was air-borne, but our epidemiologists and infection control people said: "It may be air-borne but it really doesn't look like it, so let's assume it's contact-based and put in all the necessary precautions for that." So we were all told to wear what we called "M3G" – mask, gown, gloves and goggles. After we instituted this, the rate of transmission between staff and patients dropped. In hindsight, this saved us. But we could have been wrong.

We could never let our guard down, even when we went on breaks to the tea room to eat or rest. A few of us might be in the room together, but we would always leave some distance between us, in case one of us was harbouring it. That kind of alertness is very mentally draining, so that's why when we finally had zero Sars cases, we were all kind of emotionless. We were just exhausted. We also sometimes had the feeling that we shouldn't celebrate too early, because you never knew what the next week would bring.

It's hard to talk about it even now, because looking back, a lot of things come back to me – some good, some very hard, but all of it life-altering.

Tan Tock Seng Hospital was Sars Central in Singapore. It was where the Health Ministry decided to centralise all patients of the deadly disease in the second month of its spread. Patients had to be isolated in the hospital's ICU wards, which Dr Tai Hwei Yee was in charge of.

I had no shoes to go to school in

Olivia Lum, 54, overcame a tough childhood to later start her water treatment company Hyflux.
It listed on the Singapore Exchange in 2001 and is now a leading global desalination operation

Someone told me that I was abandoned as a baby at the hospital by my neighbours. I can't verify this because the woman who adopted me would never tell me. She adopted four other children, and we lived in a village house in Kampar, Ipoh, that had no electricity and no water. Every morning I had to walk 50m to get water from a well and every night I had to pump kerosene to light lamps. I hated doing both these things. It took a lot of strength to pump kerosene, and the lamp would last only two hours. So I made sure to complete my homework within the two hours.

My siblings and I went to school in slippers because we couldn't afford school shoes. I was weak because of malnutrition and couldn't do PE, until in Primary 3 I found out that Sports Day was where all the prizes were – and the prizes were shoes, towels and soap. So the next year, I tied some sandbags around my ankles that I had sewn myself and ran around my compound every morning before school started. In Primary 4, I took part in three events – 100m, 4x100m and long jump. I ran barefoot, but I won all three. I got so many prizes! I took them home and my whole family had new things. The Lux soap was such a luxury. The first time we used it, our toilet smelt so fresh. And that first time we had new Bata shoes – that kind of joy, I cannot tell you. So I decided I had to take part every year.

My whole neighbourhood was trapped in a poverty cycle. Most people dropped out of school after primary school and were involved in drugs and gangs. I was always looking for some kind of hope as a child and always asked my teacher: "How do I become like you?" His only answer: "Study hard." So that stuck in my head.

When I was 15, I topped my town in a national exam. My principal told me: "This place is too small for you. Go to KL or Singapore." I had some female neighbours who had gone to Singapore as construction workers. They kindly took me in. So while I was looking for a school, I was staying in a small room with eight construction workers.

None of the schools in Singapore wanted me because I had a Malaysian certificate. I was about to give up and go back to Malaysia when the bus I was on passed Tiong Bahru Secondary School. I thought I'd give it one last try. The principal there was touched after hearing my story. He asked me to return another day to take an entrance exam. I said: "Can I take it right now?" I was so afraid he would change his mind. So I took three tests – English, Maths and Science – there and then. He said: "Your results are quite good! I think we can accept you."

I went on to Hwa Chong and NUS, and after university I started working as a chemist at Glaxo Pharmaceuticals. I loved science and I had a well-paying job, but ever since I was a kid, I had admired people doing business. So in 1984, I resigned to start my own waste water treatment business. I sold my little apartment in Bayshore and my Nissan Sunny so I could rent a room in an HDB flat, a factory in Tampines, and buy a motorcycle. When you're a one-man show, you don't even dare pay yourself, so my classmates became my benefactors. I'd ask them to buy me lunch.

It was very tough at first because I was a nobody in Singapore. Customers would say, why should I buy from you? How do I know you won't go bankrupt tomorrow? So in the end, I rode my motorcycle to visit Malaysian factories. When people saw the Singapore address on my card, they thought I must be some kind of MNC, because I was a cross-country company. So they accepted me, and that's how I started my business – from Malaysia first.

I happened to catch the right wave and listed Hyflux in 2001, just when Singapore started to want to be self-sufficient in water. The initial public offering gave us a huge boost and we were able to do much larger projects – we won four of the five big municipal projects that the Public Utilities Board launched.

Miracle after miracle – that's how I got to where I am today. After the IPO, I felt that I'd managed to make it, but I still wanted to find my siblings. So I put ads in the Chinese dailies in Singapore and Malaysia. Within a month I received their calls. They were all still quite poor then, labourers and construction workers. It was such a happy reunion, and now I gather them once a year in Singapore.

Olivia Lum is the founder, executive chairman and group chief executive of Hyflux, a leading water treatment company in Asia with projects in Southeast Asia, China, India, Algeria, the Middle East and North Africa. She was the first Singaporean and first woman to be named the Ernst & Young World Entrepreneur of the Year in 2011.

Fast worker
keeps cargo flowing

As one of PSA's elite quay crane operators, Tommy Lim Chee Kiang, 48,
has soared ahead in his work since joining as a truck driver in 1997

I am a quay crane operator for PSA Singapore Terminals. The faster I can unload the containers, and safely, the more incentive payments I'll get as a reward. At my best, I can complete one move – unloading a container and setting it on a container truck, for instance – within a minute. In a single day, I can move up to 200 containers.

I have to look out for the wharf supervisors below my crane, who make sure the instructions from the control centre are carried out correctly, as well as the container truck drivers. I must focus in order to carry out my moves safely and accurately, so I can avoid accidents. Even though I sit alone in my crane for eight hours every shift, I am not lonely, because I am always on the radio with them.

My crane cabin, which has the floor area of a king-sized bed, has a clear glass bottom and windows all around. I have two computer screens that show instructions from the control centre, and two panels of gears and buttons beside me to control the crane. It is a bit like controlling a computer game. The quay cranes are between 10 and 15 storeys high – you can't be afraid of heights to do this job. From this height, you have the best view of the steady stream of ships that come into the port. You can also catch the sunrise on the morning or overnight shifts, and the sunset on the afternoon shift.

The best part of the job is that I have made a lot of friends, with whom I have learnt to work as a team. After work, some play soccer and I watch, or we have a drinking session, or we go for movies.

Having been with PSA for 18 years since 1997, I have seen the port grow from handling 14 million TEUs – 20-foot equivalent units, used to describe the capacity of container ships and terminals based on the volume of a 20-foot-long container – to 32 million TEUs last year. I, too, have grown with the company.

Before I joined PSA, I helped my elderly parents with their chicken rice stall. My mother, who knew I did not enjoy studying and was worried I would not find a job, insisted I learn to drive at the age of 18, so I would have a skill. I had completed my O levels and decided that was enough. After my parents retired in 1997, I responded to an advertisement in *The Straits Times* for the job of a container truck driver with PSA, because I enjoy driving.

But I wanted better pay, and upgraded my skills so that I could become a yard crane operator, and later a quay crane operator, considered the "elite" of container equipment specialists. PSA has 2,400 container equipment specialists, of whom 30 per cent are quay crane operators. A yard crane operator just starting out at PSA can earn about $2,600 monthly, but quay crane operators receive a special skills allowance on top of our monthly salary.

I live in a five-room HDB flat in Woodlands and am married with two children. My son, 22, has just completed National Service after attending the Institute of Technical Education, while my daughter, 21, is completing her final year in polytechnic. My mother, who died in 2009, would feel comforted over what I have achieved. It is because of her I got my driving licence, and have what I have today.

Tommy Lim Chee Kiang may be alone in his crane cabin for eight hours every shift, but says he does not feel lonely, as he is always communicating with port colleagues who help him do his job.

Jailed 8 times, and a manager now

Angel Ng, 50, was in and out of jail for drug offences between 1982 and 2008. The Yellow Ribbon Project, launched in 2004, put her on her feet. She now manages three call centres

Being in and out of jail so many times since I was 17 did not scare me off prison life. Being in prison was no big deal; some prisoners wanted to return to prison because they found that better than having to face society.

In 1994, two weeks after I gave birth to my only child, Valerie, I was jailed yet again. I'm aggressive and argumentative by nature and I'd always had the spirit of *buay sai see* (must not die). But this time, I had post-natal depression, missed my baby and was worried about how my mother, who'd just been told she had cervical cancer, would cope with bringing up Valerie.

One day, when I was punished with solitary confinement, I thought: "I've been such a burden to my mother, and I can't change. It's best to end it all." I took a metal spike from the toilet brush and cut my wrists. But I hadn't sharpened the spike, so the cuts weren't deep enough to kill me quickly. The wardens saved me.

Still, I was not motivated to change my ways. I just wanted to damage myself completely because I had a deep anger against the world for being unwanted from birth. Every time I was released from prison, I could work only in nightclubs where I was always with people in the drugs business. I had no one to tell me how to break this self-destructive cycle.

While in prison, at the age of 33, I managed to study for O levels and scored five straight A1s in subjects like English Literature and History.

In 2003, when I was 38 and started serving my longest-ever prison sentence – eight and a half years, later reduced to six – I began reading books on religion and philosophy from the prison library. Age was catching up with me. I thought: "I can't keep living like this."

The following year, I learnt that the prison authorities were starting Asia's first prison call centre, part of the Yellow Ribbon Project that had just been set up to help ex-offenders find jobs to reintegrate into society. I wanted to work there because it was a white-collar job for which I only had to use my voice, and not my physical appearance. So I'd be able to work till I was very old.

But the prison authorities kept saying: "This job is not for hardcore folk like you." I would reply: "It's hardcore people like me who need this opportunity."

Then, in 2006, they didn't have enough staff for the centre. So they interviewed me and I got a job selling health supplements. I was blessed to work with a buddy, Denise, who was well-educated and spoke very professionally to callers. I wrote down every word she said. I also read up on supplements in the prison library. Within three months, I was the centre's top seller.

I was released from my last prison term on 11 November 2008, and, a week later, began working at Connect Centre's headquarters outside the prison. It's been a big learning experience for me, and it's taken me to new places. For example, when I do presentations, I don't get stage fright because of my years as a nightclub singer, but I'm still pressured when people ask me questions in front of everyone else. But by God's grace, I have managed to overcome my fears and sense of inferiority.

Some organisations have supported Connect's business a lot, including the doctors' hotline Synapse, L'Oreal Singapore and the Singapore Academy of Law. I tell the academy: "My colleagues and I were once law abusers; now we serve those with queries about law events."

The government could give ex-offenders more help in resolving real-life concerns. In prison, they don't have to pay bills or wash their clothes. Meals are provided. But on their release, everything is money and responsibility.

Most newly released ex-offenders have no money, so Connect gives them $10 a day for meals until they get their first month's pay of about $1,000. They need to stay focused by holding a steady job because that disciplines and stabilises them. I tell them: "Commit to your job. Don't look for loopholes. After work, spend time with your family. Contribute to your family's expenses or buy them small things they like. That's how you regain their trust."

Today, my daughter teaches children with severe autism at the Asian Women's Welfare Association. I'm glad she has a caring heart and a sense of responsibility.

Call centre general manager Angel Ng oversees more than 50 colleagues – mostly ex-offenders – at Connect Centre, which trains ex-offenders here to run its three call centres professionally so they can hold down steady jobs and fit into society once more.

From Redman syrup to Norwegian marzipan

Wong Chen Liong, 67, who supplies baking and dessert ingredients, has had to keep up with Singaporeans' increasingly sophisticated tastes

Over the 50 years I have been in Phoon Huat, I have seen how Singaporeans' tastes for dessert have changed. When my brother developed our Redman flavoured concentrates in 1968, they were very popular. These concentrates, in 13 flavours such as orange, lime and grape, can be mixed with water and sugar. It was an affordable way to add flavour to plain water, and did not require refrigeration.

Today, it is easier to pop open a can of chilled soda.

Dessert fads have come and gone: black forest cakes, Japanese cheesecakes, mousse cakes, Konnyaku jelly – and now it's cupcakes. From sponge cakes topped with whipped cream, Singaporeans now prepare a wide range of sophisticated desserts, from cream puffs and chocolate brownies to tiramisu and crème brûlée.

As Singapore progressed and people became wealthier, more people became willing to spend on desserts, and as a result, our customer base has grown. Phoon Huat has also grown to meet our customers' needs. When we first started in 1947, my father Wong Tai Fuang stocked only a handful of products – non-refrigerated margarine, dried fruits, baking powder, food colouring and flavouring, and baking cases – all imported from England, since Singapore was a British colony.

Sixty-eight years on, we stock over 3,000 products from at least 30 countries, including olive oil from Spain, marzipan from Norway, dairy whipping cream and frozen fruits from France, cherries, almonds and walnuts from America, and glazing gel from Belgium.

Phoon Huat, so named because my father believed you have to "put in effort" (*phoon* in Hainanese) in order to be "prosperous" (*huat*), now has 12 branches, from Bencoolen Street to Buona Vista. We are also a wholesaler to ship chandlers, hotels and airline caterers, and export products to nearby countries.

We started out in a 35 sq m shop in Middle Road. My father, then a waiter, learnt about baking ingredients and food colouring from a distant granduncle in Butterworth, Malaysia.

After the war, many Hainanese cooks who had worked for the British began striking out on their own, selling cookies, butter cakes and fruit cakes. Many Hainanese also owned coffeeshops, bakeries and steakhouses. My father saw an opportunity to supply them with the ingredients they would need.

My eldest brother Chin Wee, then 16, helped out at the shop, while my second brother Chen Keng, who is four years younger, also joined the business a few years later. I was born in 1948, after my mother had three girls here, and joined my father as a delivery man at the age of 16.

We have been able to do well because our country enjoys good leadership and an open port, which allows us to import all sorts of ingredients without encountering much red tape.

I used to live in a single house of seven rooms, two bathrooms and one water closet with more than 10 other families in the city. The men would do their business in the sandy alley behind the house, where the children played. And if our marbles rolled onto the waste, we would just wash it off and continue playing.

Today, I live with my family in a condominium in central Singapore. I am married with four children and seven grandchildren.

All in the family business are (from left) Wong Chen Liong, brother Wong Chen Keng and nephew John Wong, who help run Phoon Huat. The company, best known for its Redman syrups in its early days, has expanded its product range to include marzipan from Norway and glazing gel from Belgium.

My son, award-winning Pathlight artist

Sales engineer Kelvin Phua, 55, talks about his son Glenn, 19, who has autism and has been dubbed Singapore's Stephen Wiltshire

During Glenn's school holidays in 2010, when he was 14, we found a note in his schoolbag about some art homework he had to submit. It had to be related to F1, and he drew eight cars coming around a race track. We didn't pay much attention to it, except to say "Good job". We were just happy he had finished his homework.

A few months later, his school, Pathlight School, called us and said: "Your son has won a big prize." We had no idea what this was about, but took leave to attend the ceremony in Raffles Place. Only when we were there did we realise he had won first prize – a set of F1 tickets for four people for three days, for seats with a very nice view, and an opportunity for Glenn to sit in a real F1 car.

After that, Glenn's art teacher realised his talent and the school set up an art development programme, partly because of him.

We discovered he was autistic when he was four, when he had trouble making eye contact. He attended a mainstream primary school until halfway through Primary 2, when he couldn't keep up. We got him into Pathlight, which teaches a mainstream curriculum and life skills to children with autism, and which opened in 2004. Life with him was very frustrating. As a small example, if someone said "Good morning" to you 20 different times, every single morning, wouldn't you get annoyed, too?

After he started attending Pathlight, I attended an anger management class that the school organised. I started trying some of the strategies, and also swapped notes with his teachers about what works for Glenn. But you know, if you don't love your kid, no one will love your kid. It's not about giving in to everything he wants, but about managing your own temper and behaviour, and learning what works and what doesn't with him. We had a hard time with him, but children with autism are also the most loving.

We didn't actually realise he had this talent. When he was about eight or nine, he drew a lot of cartoons, copying characters from *Peanuts* or *The Simpsons*, and they were very good, but we didn't think much of this, because all children doodle. Around that age, he attended an art course at a community centre and the teacher said: "Your son doesn't draw well." So we didn't send him to any other classes.

But since he won the F1 competition, he has drawn more than 150 pictures, mostly of buildings. After a certain age, he stopped liking pencils. Now he uses drawing pens. He never sketches – he just puts pen to paper and draws. If he makes a mistake, he'll find a way to modify it to still make it part of the picture.

His drawings are extremely detailed. He takes about 20 to 25 hours on average with each one. He doesn't draw from memory or on the spot – he finds it too hot to draw outdoors, and needs a desk. He always works from a photograph. His process is very complex; he doesn't draw from left to right, but he'll jump around the picture. Sometimes I'll watch him working, and I'll see something random, and I'll ask him – is that a mistake? But he'll say: "Daddy, that's my starting point." When he's done with the picture, you'll have no idea where he started.

At a Pathlight parents' communication night, Member of Parliament Denise Phua, who helped set up the school, called Glenn "the Stephen Wiltshire of Singapore", referring to the famous British artist who has autism. We were so proud.

Glenn's drawings are sold at the Pathlight Mall and also auctioned for charity events. He's made more than $10,000 from the sales of his art. Some teachers at his school say: "Better buy now because the price will only go up." But he has no idea his drawings are quite well-known. He has a very pure heart. We encourage him, and he knows he'll get compliments if he finishes a drawing, but that's all.

When Glenn was younger, we would think about his future and feel lost. Now, we're definitely more confident of his future. Pathlight has recently set up an art gallery for its artists, which also sells works by students who have graduated. It feels like there's a direction for Glenn now, and he can earn a living.

Glenn Phua, seen here with his father Kelvin, was found to be autistic when he was four. His talent as an artist was discovered later when he won an art competition. His original drawings sell for as much as $5,000 each and have been auctioned at charity galas. Two of Glenn's drawings can be seen on the inside front and back covers of this book.

The Singapore Dress

Several local designers, asked to come up with a look that Singapore women can call their own, sketched these creations

A reflection of the country's multicultural identity, Singapore fashion is a deep fusion of East, West, North and South. We live in an open society where everything is accepted, with Indians, Malays and Chinese coexisting harmoniously. The Singapore national dress to me should be a kaleidoscopic reflection of all these cultures. I hope that with these unique elements, Singapore fashion will get more global attention.

Frederick Lee, 42

Photo from AFTON CHEN

It is a two-piece outfit comprising a fitted, soft-tailored jacket that is cinched at the waist with a gold belt. The front of the jacket should be held together with the kerongsang, a set of three jewelled brooches used to fasten a Malay or Peranakan woman's tunic. The first two gold brooches should be of a simpler and smaller design, and the third gold brooch should be modelled after our national flower, Vanda Miss Joaquim. The skirt has a base silhouette of a fitted cheongsam, a body-hugging traditional dress for Chinese women, and an outer silk drape with pleating that is reminiscent of the sari. The design is modern yet retains key features of the different traditional costumes of the main ethnic groups.

Afton Chen, 29, of Reckless Erica

All photos from
SINGAPORE PRESS HOLDINGS
(unless otherwise indicated)

The name of this design, *Progress*, is inspired by the last line of our national pledge, "so as to achieve happiness, prosperity and progress for our nation". And to show that Singapore is a city of rapid change and transformation, this piece is created as a transformable gown. With a simple release of buttons, the monochromatic white piece cascades into a maxi dress that reveals laser cut-out patterns that represent the multicultural fabric of Singapore. The transformation also signifies that while Singapore is a progressive and avant garde city, it's the cultures and people that are the core of nation-building.

Kenny Lim, 38 (left), and Andrew Loh, 40, of Depression

The print is entitled *HDB BLOCK* and is taken from my autumn/winter 2013 Heartland collection, which takes its inspiration from old-fashioned HDB blocks. We share similar cultures with our neighbouring countries, but the HDB block is truly a Singaporean creation and is a perfect symbol of our nation-building. The pattern is developed from my hand-drawn artwork, which shows the façade of low-rise HDB blocks found in Siglap. The dress shape hints at our iconic Singapore Girl uniform, but is shortened to the knee for a modern look that reflects our society.

Jo Soh, 39, of Hansel

The inspiration behind the design is based on a forward and modern Singapore. The design approach is a combination of pleating and slightly cinched waist to give it a more feminine look. Red as a bold choice of colour represents prosperity and good fortune for the nation, and we hope this dress reflects the ambition we have, likewise, for our national flag.

Nic Wong, 42, of Saturday

1995 — 2004

| 1995 | 1996 | 1997 | 1998 | 1999 |

- Rogue trader **Nick Leeson** brings down Britain's oldest merchant bank, Barings, on 27 February; he is jailed for 6½ years here

- On 1 March, a **Family Court** is set up to hear most family-related disputes; this evolves into the Family Justice Court in 2014

- Free-to-air television channels TCS5 and TCS8 begin **round-the-clock transmission** from 27 September

- On 2 November, Parliament passes the **Maintenance of Parents Bill**, mooted by Nominated MP Walter Woon, which gives destitute people the right to demand financial support from their children

- Singapore is **no longer a developing country**, says the Organisation for Economic Cooperation and Development in January; the nation's per capita GDP is now US$20,000, the 16th highest in the world

- All Singaporean children born on or after 2 January must have **at least six years of formal education**

- Fandi Ahmad, **Singapore's first millionaire sportsman**, marries South African model Wendy Jacobs on 5 December; they go on to have five children

- Homegrown TV drama *Growing Up* debuts. It runs for six seasons, making it Singapore's **longest-running English TV drama**

- On 17 May, **National Education** is introduced in schools here to foster a shared sense of nationhood among young Singaporeans

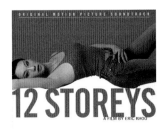

- Also in May, film-maker Eric Khoo is the first Singaporean to have his movie, *12 Storeys*, screened at the Cannes Film Festival

- On 26 September, 29 sailors go missing at sea after **two ships collide** in the Straits of Malacca after the yearly haze, with a record Pollutant Standards Index reading of 226, hampers visibility

- All 104 people on board Silkair Flight **MI185** are killed on 19 December when the plane plunges into Indonesia's Musi River

- On 2 January, the **Second Link** connecting Tuas to Tanjung Kupang in Johor opens; the 2km or so bridge is meant to ease congestion at the Causeway

- Local sitcom **Phua Chu Kang Pte Ltd** makes TV history here when its entire 20-episode first season is re-run on 12 February, after its debut on 2 October 1997

Photo from 1ST SINGAPORE EVEREST TEAM

- On 25 May, Edwin Siew and Khoo Swee Chiow of the **Singapore Everest Team** are the first to unfurl the Singapore flag on the world's highest peak

- Physics teacher and former Barisan Sosialis MP for Jurong **Chia Thye Poh**, 57, is freed unconditionally after being detained under the Internal Security Act in 1966

- On 1 April, the 3.5 sq m **landfill on Pulau Semakau** opens. It is today Singapore's lone landfill and an unlikely global icon for biodiversity

- On 1 September, **SR Nathan** is sworn in as Singapore's sixth president after he is uncontested in the presidential election; he becomes the nation's longest-serving president after two further uncontested terms

- On 6 September, lawmakers here walk over from the old Parliament House, built in 1826, to its locally designed and built replacement in nearby **Parliament Place**

Despite a hiccup brought on by the Asian Financial Crisis,
Singapore is now among the world's richest countries

2000

- A demonstration **NEWater plant** opens in Bedok in May, using new technology to recycle waste water. The first full-fledged NEWater plant opens in Bedok in February 2003

- On 1 September, **Speakers' Corner** opens at Hong Lim Park, with self-employed Lim Kian Heng, 40, the first to hold court there

- The billion-dollar petrochemical hub **Jurong Island** opens officially on 14 October, five years after seven islets were joined to create it; the entire 30 sq m island is completed on 25 September 2009

- Eighty-three among the 179 people on board Singapore Airlines Flight **SQ006** are killed on 31 October when the plane smashes into construction equipment on take-off from Taipei's international airport

2001

- On 1 April, the government introduces the **Baby Bonus Scheme** to lighten the financial load of married couples who want big families

- On 8 April, after a 97-hour operation, surgeons Keith Goh and Chumpon Chan **separate conjoined Nepalese twins** Ganga (left) and Jamuna Shrestha; Ganga dies of meningitis on 29 July 2008

- The **Internal Security Department arrests** 13 members of regional Islamic militant group Jemaah Islamiyah and two others, thwarting their plan to carry out a series of bombings on several diplomatic missions in Singapore. Other targets included Yishun MRT station

2002

- On 14 January, thanks to awareness raised by nature lovers here, the government postpones the reclamation of Pulau Ubin to preserve its **Chek Jawa** beach, which is home to many, often rare, wildlife species

- On 19 May, Singapore's **first air-conditioned bus interchange** opens at Toa Payoh

- On 12 October, the $600 million **Esplanade – Theatres on the Bay** opens; by 2014, the performing arts centre has staged more than 25,000 shows and drawn more than 18.5 million people

2003

- Thirty-three people here die of the pneumonia pandemic known as **Severe Acute Respiratory Syndrome**, or Sars, between 1 March and 16 July, with another 238 surviving the virus, which brings business here almost to a standstill

- On 20 June, the **North-East Line** opens here as the world's first driverless, fully underground heavy train line, with 16 stations over 20km

- On 29 October, Singapore's first biomedical park, the $500 million **Biopolis**, opens; the 185,000 sq m development houses 2,000 international scientists and is an icon of the nation's $1 billion push towards R&D since 2000

2004

- **Lee Hsien Loong** is the country's third premier, succeeding his predecessor Goh Chok Tong on 12 August

- More than 230,000 people die on or after 26 December, when massive waves from a **tsunami** slam the coasts of countries encircling the Indian Ocean. Singaporeans respond strongly in cash and kind, including aiding victims in Indonesia's Aceh province

- In December, **National Service is reduced** to two years, from the 2½-year term set in 1971

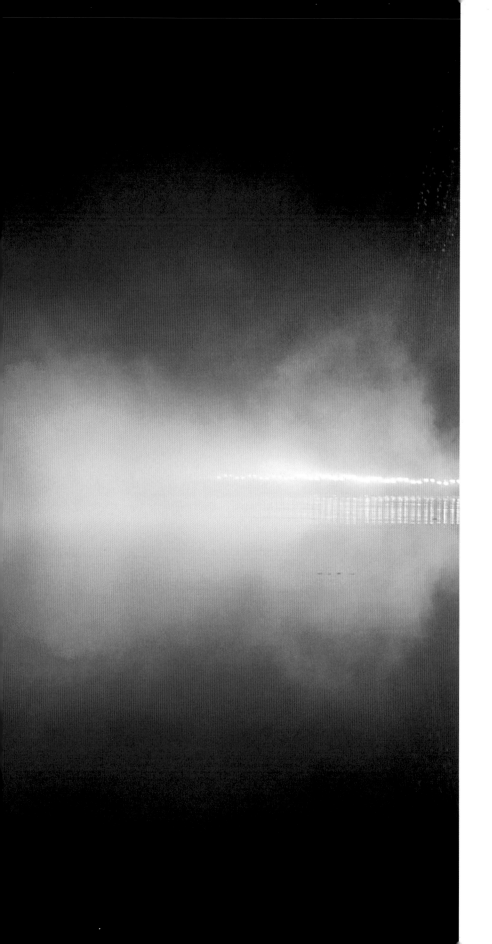

A NATION RACES ON

National sailor Darren Choy running towards the 30m-high cauldron at the opening ceremony of the Youth Olympic Games in 2010. Singapore was the host of the inaugural Games.

Photo by SAMUEL HE

She was told to switch from the track to the catwalk, but Dipna Lim Prasad persisted and went on to win the bronze medal for 400m hurdles at the SEA Games in Myanmar in 2013.

Team Singapore athletes and officials, past and present, gather at the National Stadium for a tribute photograph

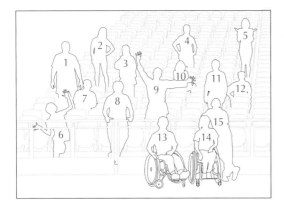

1. James Wong, 46 (athletics). 10-time SEA Games gold medallist (1993–2011). Sportsman of the Year (2004)

2. Savannah Siew, 19 (sailing). 2014 Asian Games gold medallist and 2014 420 Ladies World Championships silver medallist

3. Sheik Alaud'din, 48 (silat). 13 national titles, 2-time world champion, 2-time World Invitation champion, 3-time SEA Games champion, 3-time Coach of the Year (1999, 2001, 2002)

4. Zainal Abidin, 57 (squash). 11-time national champion from 1977 to 1986, 9-time East Asian Champion. Sportsman of the Year (1987)

5. Saiyidah Aisyah, 27 (rowing). First individual gold medallist for rowing at 2013 SEA Games

6. Laurentia Tan, 36 (para equestrian). 2-time Paralympian. Won 3 bronzes and 1 silver at the Paralympic Games

7. Neo Beng Siang, 48 (basketball). Head coach, national team and Singapore Slingers. Delivered first basketball medal after 34 years at 2013 SEA Games

8. Quah Kim Song, 63 (football). Played in national team from 1969 to 1981. Led the team to Malaysia Cup victory in 1977 after 12-year drought

9. Muhammad Shakir Juanda, 27 (silat). Champion at 2012 World Pencak Silat Championships

10. Grace Young, 53 (bowling). Multiple Asian and international titles. 3-time national champion. Sportswoman of the Year (1990, 1992, 1993)

11. Tan Eng Bock, 79 (waterpolo). Olympian and member of team that won the only Asian Games gold medal, in 1954. National coach with 9 SEA Games golds from 1970 to 1990 and 6 times Team of the Year. Coach of the Year (1976)

12. SS Dhillon, 84 (official). First and longest-serving secretary-general of Singapore National Olympic Council (1971–1996). Developed selection criteria for participation at major Games and Multi-Million-Dollar Awards Programme

13. Robert Tan, 68 (para sports). Represented Singapore in athletics, archery, basketball, bodybuilding, fencing and weightlifting. Still competing in lawn bowls

14. Yip Pin Xiu, 23 (para swimming). 2-time Paralympian and Singapore's first Paralympic gold winner. Won gold and silver in 50m backstroke and 50m freestyle respectively at 2008 Beijing Paralympics

15. C Kunalan, 73 (athletics). 2-time Olympian. Won 5 Asian Games medals and 15 SEA Games medals. Held national record for 100m for 33 years. Sportsman of the Year (1969, 1970)

On the right track, after all

Everyone told her to quit because she was too slow at running, but hurdler
Dipna Lim Prasad, 24, went on to be a national record-breaker

When I was in Primary 5, my track and field teammates once shouted at me to quit because I was very slow compared to them.

In 2011, a coach at an Asian track competition told me I should quit because there was no hope for me. He told me to be a model instead.

Even my mother wanted me to quit – although she told me this only recently. It made her sad to see me crying every time I lost.

But I refused to give up.

I just loved running. I loved playing catching with my neighbourhood friends as a young girl, and I loved running more than I felt terrible about my losses. So I kept on. I thought I was on the right track when I made it to the pioneer batch of students at the Singapore Sports School in 2004.

My breakthrough came in 2013 when I broke the women's 200m national record, which had stood for 29 years. In the same year, I won the bronze medal for 400m hurdles at the Southeast Asian (SEA) Games in Myanmar. I now hold the women's 400m hurdles national record.

All this wouldn't have been possible if it weren't for my coach Viatcheslav Vassiliev, "Coach Slava", who introduced me to hurdles at the age of 16 in 2007, when I was a student at the sports school.

I resisted switching to hurdles. I was already getting faster, shaving six seconds off my 400m sprint in Secondary 2 in 2005 to win gold at the National Schools competition. I thought, why fix what's not broken?

But Coach Slava told me hurdles would help my sprint event because it requires more perfection in your rhythm and strides. He was right.

In 2012, I went to the London Olympics on a wild card, and ran next to one of Australia's greatest Olympians, Sally Pearson, in the 100m hurdles in the heats. It was such a good experience seeing how she had the mental focus to tune out the crowds, the cameras and any harassment she faced to win the gold medal. It made me realise what was required of world-class athletes.

Since graduating from Nanyang Technological University with a degree in sports science and management, I've been training for global competitions with sponsorships from Tiger Balm and Nike, and a stipend from Sport Singapore. I have my sights set on the gold medal in the 400m hurdles event at the SEA Games this year and qualifying for the 400m hurdles at the Olympics in Rio de Janeiro next year. If I make it, I'd be the first Singaporean to do so.

But even if I never win a gold medal at the Olympics, I know I am not wasting my time. As I got better, people began telling me I was making a positive difference. One person said I motivated her daughter to join track. Another girl made her mother buy her sports shoes after attending a talk I gave at my alma mater, St Nicholas Girls' School.

I think people can relate to my story because I didn't just put on my spike shoes and win. I was really bad, and I'm proof that if you suck at something, you should just keep trying, because you *can* get better.

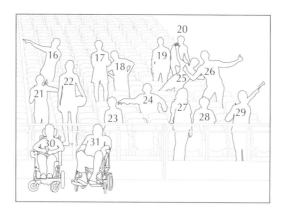

16 Lee Wung Yew, 49 (shooting). 3-time Olympian. Won 16 golds, 2 silvers and 3 bronzes at SEA Games. Sportsman of the Year (1990, 1998)

17 Feng Tianwei, 29 (table-tennis). 2-time Olympian. Singapore's most bemedalled Olympian with 1 silver and 2 bronzes. Sportswoman of the Year (2010, 2013)

18 Jing Jun Hong, 46 (table-tennis). 3-time Olympian. Won 2 Commonwealth Games golds. Sportswoman of the Year (1997, 1998, 2001). Head coach of national team

19 Joscelin Yeo, 36 (swimming). 4-time Olympian. Won most number of SEA Games gold medals (40). Sportswoman of the Year (1994, 1996, 2000)

20 Syed Abdul Kadir, 67 (boxing). Olympian and only local boxer to win a Commonwealth Games bronze medal, in 1974. Sportsman of the Year (1975). Coach of the Year (1985)

21 Veronica Shanti Pereira, 19 (athletics). National record-holder for women's 100m and 200m events

22 Micky Lin, 30 (netball). National team captain. Led the team to defend Asian Netball Championships title in 2014

23 Tan Yoon Yin, 86 (official). Founder of Singapore Women's Hockey Association and Singapore Women's Netball Association (now known as Netball Singapore)

24 Majid Ariff, 81 (football). One of the greatest footballers in Singapore. Discovered and nurtured many local football stars including Fandi Ahmad

25 Melanie Martens, 55 (hockey). Named in the Asian All-Star team in 1994. National team captain, scored penalty goal at 1993 SEA Games to win gold

26 Eugene Teo, 28 (waterpolo). National team captain. Singapore has won 25 golds in a row at the SEAP/SEA Games

27 Annabel Pennefather, 66 (hockey). Represented Singapore from 1964 to 1980. First Asian woman elected vice-president of International Hockey Federation. Technical official at the Sydney Olympics. SNOC vice-president

28 Tang Pui Wah, 82 (athletics). Singapore's first female Olympian in athletics

29 Jasmine Ser, 25 (shooting). Olympian and Asian Games silver medallist in 2006 and Commonwealth Games gold medallist in 2010 and 2014. Sportswoman of the Year (2011)

30 Nurulasyiqah Mohammad Taha, 30 (boccia). First Singaporean to qualify for boccia in 2012 London Paralympics

31 Arumugam Vijiaratnam, 94 (hockey). Singapore's oldest surviving Olympian. Represented Singapore in cricket, football, hockey and rugby in international tournaments

Struck by lightning and I felt I was stuck on a different planet

Carolyn Lim, 37, who uses a wheelchair after a lightning strike, says although more people are aware of the disabled now, things can still be improved

My life changed dramatically when I was 28 after I was struck by lightning on 10 September 2006. My friends and I had been windsurfing off East Coast Park when it started to rain. We began heading back to shore when suddenly, lightning struck. Then, someone spotted me floating face down in the water.

Until then, I had been a teacher who spent my free time rollerblading, windsurfing, dancing or working out at the gym. When I awoke from a six-week coma, nothing was the same. I could not speak, walk or write. I became depressed.

It wasn't until my boyfriend William proposed to me six months later that I realised I needed to start living again. I taught myself to speak by reading books aloud, sometimes taking an entire month to finish one story. I also trained my right hand, which had lost all fine motor skills, to pick up simple items: first a spoon, then a fork, then chopsticks. Now I can type.

I can also walk slowly. I try to practise in my room daily, but I cannot balance well, so I still rely on a wheelchair to get around in public. My doctor says I have to keep practising these skills, or I will lose them. It has something to do with how a certain part of my brain was injured during the incident.

But I have done my best to move on. William and I got married in 2007, and we now have two sons, Isaac, five, and Asher, two. In 2009, I completed a master's degree in education with the National Institute of Education, and launched a book, *Making Pink Lemonade*, about my struggle against adversity. I now do freelance work writing specimen exam papers for a publisher.

My condition also opened me up to a way of life that I never gave much thought to before: I was now a wheelchair-bound Singaporean. I can joke about it now, but when I first started going out after the accident, I could feel every look and stare that people gave me.

Once, while I was waiting for the lift at an HDB block, a young boy who saw me asked the adult with him: "Is that contagious?" A part of me wanted to hit the boy, and another part of me wanted to crawl into a corner. It was a traumatic experience, and showed me that Singaporeans then lacked exposure and didn't know much about people with disabilities.

People are now more aware about disabled individuals and their needs, so unpleasant incidents happen less often. While there are still people who aren't the nicest and abuse facilities for the disabled, this can be changed by education.

There are still some issues, though, with building and infrastructure, such as toilets, carparks and sheltered walkways. One hotel in town had a handicapped parking space in the basement carpark, but no lift to the hotel lobby – only stairs. Then there are carparks that have a reserved parking space and a ramp, but a heavy push-pull glass door at the entrance. Recently, I got stranded at a park near my home when it rained because some of the ramps aren't sheltered.

These encounters really made me feel that society was unfriendly and alienating. I felt stuck on a different planet, where I was just an afterthought. Singapore is an ageing society and we are going to have more old people in wheelchairs. More thought and effort need to be put into these things. Addressing these issues would require a change in the mindset of planners and architects.

But I've also met many lovely people. I've lost count of the number of people who held doors open for us and rushed to help when they saw me trying to climb stairs with William's help. These include parents with their arms full of toddlers and aunties with bulging shopping trolleys.

I recently watched a TED talk by disability advocate Stella Young. She talks about how disabled people in wheelchairs should not be exceptional. I agree. The day the disabled and the wheelchair-users stop being the exception, that's the day when all these issues will disappear.

A young boy who saw Carolyn Lim in a wheelchair asked: "Is that contagious?" But she says Singaporeans are now more aware about disabled people.

Helping a disabled hawker cook *nasi lemak*

Social entrepreneur Koh Seng Choon, 56, founded Dignity Kitchen, a food court and hawker training school for the disabled and disadvantaged

I was executive director of the Restaurant Association of Singapore in 2005 and we were running courses for chefs when a man with polio came to see me, saying: "I want to be a chef." I told him: "Even if I train you, it'll be hard. If you know the way restaurants are run, there are different layers. You'll be going in as a kitchen helper, washing plates and bowls. You have polio. How are you going to do it?"

But that's how the idea for Dignity Kitchen came about. In a restaurant you need to train a guy to cook many things, but in a hawker centre, I just need to train him to cook one thing, like *bak chor mee* or *rojak*, really well.

The idea is very simple: You train disabled people to cook hawker food – and when I refer to disability, I mean physical, mental, intellectual and even social disability, like battered wives and former drug addicts. It's the simplest form of enterprise. We have been able to find work for all our trainees, though for some it can take as many as 12 tries.

In 2007, with an early design of Dignity Kitchen, I went to Spring Singapore to ask for its Seed Fund. They said: "Mr Koh, your idea is very good. But you have a social angle, you should go to MCYS to get the Comcare fund." So I went to the Ministry of Community Development, Youth and Sports. They said: "Mr Koh, your idea is very good. But you have training, and that should come under WDA." So I went to the Workforce Development Authority. And do you know what they said? "Your idea is very good. But we don't fund start-ups. You should go to Spring Singapore and get the Seed Fund." One big round. But I decided to carry on.

When I looked to charities for location sites, I learnt something else. A lot of people asked me what my religion was. Does it matter? Kindness has no religion. So I decided to go commercial. That's how Dignity Kitchen started at Balestier.

In 1999, I had bought an office for my consultancy business, and by 2010, its value had doubled. I re-mortgaged it to start Dignity Kitchen. But the first batch of students couldn't deliver the goods. I had to throw away 50 chickens because they couldn't fry them, and tossed a lot of rice because they couldn't get *nasi lemak* right. That's when I asked professionals to help. I asked Thian Boon Hua, Chef Nordin, Chef Eric Teo – and everyone helped me to get it right. Then, the landlord increased rent and I had to move. I moved to Kaki Bukit, borrowing half a million dollars from two friends. After all these years, I'm finally paying them back now.

Then the rent was raised again and I moved to our current location in Serangoon in 2013. That year, my Mum died, leaving me $110,000. All the money was pumped into this place. I was still short of more than $100,000, but I was lucky that an American trust saw what I was doing and gave me the money.

When we first opened, I had the staff wear badges that labelled their disability, like "simple", or "deaf". The reason I did that was because they are very slow. They take 15 minutes to get out a bowl of noodles that you could get elsewhere in three minutes. People came, people saw, people left. Zero sales in the first 10 days. When I realised what was happening, I took all their badges. Sales picked up. But from then on, I decided, if the food is going to be slow, then it has to be very good.

Those first two years, I was losing $1,000 a day. But in 2013, my sales turnover was $1.2 million. Our costs were around $970,000. You may say, no big deal. But to me, that's a big deal! For the first time since I started Dignity Kitchen, I had a salary.

But don't measure me by my profit – measure me by my social impact. If I train one person and he gets a job for $1,000 a month, in a year that's $12,000. I've trained 300 so far. And it's not just that one person that the money affects, but his family. So that's more than $3 million worth of impact on families in a year.

My Mum and Dad taught me a simple philosophy. From age zero to 25, you learn. Get your degree, get your qualifications. From age 25 to 50, you earn: your money and your reputation. From age 50 onwards you have to return – give back. Why? The Chinese have a proverb: You come with nothing, you go with nothing. This whole thing, my whole dream, is about giving back.

Koh Seng Choon had to throw away 50 chickens because his first batch of students couldn't fry them. He also re-mortgaged an office, and used money left to him by his late mother to finance his project.

I fly and win Guinness records

Indoor skydiving is a relatively new sport involving a vertical wind tunnel, but Kyra Poh, 13, is already a world-beater

When I was in Primary 1, I drew a picture of myself flying over my school – over the basketball court, music room, art room and the pond. Maybe I always knew I was going to fly.

When my mother told me about iFly Singapore, where you can skydive indoors at Sentosa, I thought, "It can't happen, because you are defying gravity." But I got to try it at iFly in 2009. When I first got into the wind tunnel, I was laughing because I couldn't believe what was happening. It was fun. I was really happy.

I tried it with my friend Choo Yixuan, and we loved it. So we kept flying and became iFly ambassadors. We introduce iFly to friends and other first-timers, and go for international indoor skydiving competitions.

I have four official Guinness world records for indoor skydiving: the most skydiving wind tunnel verticals in a minute; the most backwards somersaults in a wind tunnel in a minute; the most passes through a hula hoop in a wind tunnel in a minute in a team of two;

and the most number of skydivers in a wind tunnel.

In 2014, I represented Singapore in the Bodyflight World Challenge in Bedford, Britain, and came in second in the Dynamic 2-Way Open category with my instructor and teammate, Kristopher Reynolds, 34.

But what I really want is to have the most number of Guinness world records. I like to win.

When I first started doing tricks like forward rolls, I'd feel nauseated. It took about two months of practice before I stopped feeling sick. Like any sport, indoor skydiving has its risks of injury, such as muscle strain or neck aches from the G-force in the tunnel. You use a lot of different muscles to stabilise yourself. But I always check with my instructor before trying anything, so the most I get are scratches if Yixuan and I don't grab each other properly in the tunnel.

My grandparents are my biggest fans. They come to watch me at every training, about three times a week. When I appear in the newspapers, my Grandpa will buy a lot of copies, laminate them and put the articles around the house. My Grandma brings me food to eat in the middle of training because you use up a lot of energy.

I know there's a really big difference between what I do for fun now, and what my parents did. My father has a woodpecker toy that he still keeps, and I think they used to play with *longkang* (drain) fish. Everybody was much closer then, and not on social media. I know I'm privileged that we have a lot of technology now, and I'm grateful.

I like visual arts and am a student at the School of the Arts. I want to be a graphic designer like my father. But I also want to intern at iFly when I'm older.

A stage voice
that's loud and clear

Actor-director Ramesh Meyyappan, 40, who was born deaf, is an internationally recognised theatre practitioner. The Singaporean, now based in Glasgow with his Scottish wife, is also a two-time Best Actor winner at the Life! Theatre Awards

When I first saw Hi! Theatre perform, I was totally in awe – a group of mostly deaf people using a language that I could totally understand, despite it not being sign language. This was the first time I thought that working in the theatre could be a real possibility for me. After that show, I met Roger Jenkins and the Hi! Theatre founders, and they encouraged me to join when I finished school.

My parents were not keen on me embarking on a life in theatre. I understood; theatre and its world were alien to them. They moved my family from India to Singapore when I was an infant, hoping we would have more opportunities, given that both my elder sister and I were deaf. They were right to do this, as we benefited from attending the Singapore School for the Deaf.

I had thought options might be limited for me, and that my future lay in some sort of nine-to-five IT job. This wasn't due to a lack of ambition – I was just being pragmatic. I do remember being drawn towards the arts in some form and I clearly enjoyed drama. I had a real desire to communicate, to tell stories.

I think I dared to dream when my friend Karen, who's now my wife, gave me the courage and self-belief to push myself a little further and direct myself towards new challenges and ideas. I met her in 1997. She saw the potential I had, but gave me a hard time, forcing me not to be complacent and pushing me to keep evolving.

The first show of mine that my parents saw was a solo performance I brought to Singapore in 2002 after I finished my studies in Liverpool. My father died a few years ago but I know he was happy for me to venture beyond Singapore. My mother now supports everything that I do, and at every one of my performances in Singapore, she is there in her best sari, smiling. My sister, who works as a school lab assistant, often comes to my shows with her three children.

Performing at the National Day Parade in 2013 is such a great memory for me. The lovely and generous Selena Tan, the creative director of the NDP that year, approached me, as she was familiar with my style of visual theatre. The idea of doing a solo piece on a big stage was scary and risky – a lot of small details of my work would be missed on a big stage. I like small, intimate venues, but I was also confident we'd create something that would translate on this big a stage. We came up with the idea of playing around with aerial work and multimedia. The two visual elements worked well together.

I remember a lot of fear leading up to that day, just thinking about being on a stage of that size, completely alone, in front of almost 40,000 people in the audience and possibly a million more watching on television. It was also terrifying climbing up the four flights of steps to get to the rope, then climbing on the rope itself at that height with the wind blowing. It was all worth it, though!

I get frustrated when deaf performers are not given the same platform as hearing performers, or are patronised. This is an attitude that is increasingly disappearing, but it isn't entirely gone. Sometimes when the deaf perform using sign language, the audience are in what I can best describe as patronising awe – they don't understand the sign but say how beautiful it is, just because it is sign.

You wouldn't expect a deaf person to say that a hearing actor is wonderful simply because he is using his voice. It is about the delivery, the emotion, the tone, the control and general expression in the voice, too.

One of my worst moments was being in a voice workshop with a tutor who had no experience at all of the deaf voice, and as a result thought that me blowing raspberries was a "breakthrough" – that he'd taught me to use my voice. We deaf have a voice that goes way beyond blowing raspberries.

Born deaf, Ramesh Meyyappan always had a desire to communicate and tell stories. He found his calling in theatre and is now an award-winning artiste, based in Glasgow.

Photo from BEN TAN PHOTOGRAPHY

"If you can get money to save animals, pigs will fly"

And that's why this hangs at my office now, says Louis Ng, 36, executive director of an animal rights group

When I wanted to start a wildlife rescue centre in 2003, a civil servant told me: "Louis, if you can get this thing going, pigs will fly. Why would the government give you land for something with no economic value in land-scarce Singapore? You've got to be crazy to even ask – and for animals, that were previously euthanised."

I tried anyway. After three years of petitioning, we received from the government a 2ha plot of land at Jalan Lekar in Choa Chu Kang. In 2009, Acres' Wildlife Rescue Centre opened its doors. I put a flying pig at the entrance of our office to show people that doing what I do is not impossible; it's just a matter of whether you want to try.

It was the same in 1999 when I first championed the end of photography sessions for baby chimpanzees at the Singapore Zoo, because they were permanently separated from their mothers and punished harshly for "not behaving". I was then a volunteer chimpanzee keeper. When I spoke up against it, the zoo fired me. Someone told me: "You're just a boy. You'll never win."

This was 16 years ago, when no one wanted to speak up about animal rights. People told me I was wasting my time – why stop something that was generating money? It took two years, and the help of British and American animal rights groups, but in 2001, the zoo ended its confinement of its "snapshot chimps" and later, its photography sessions.

I thought, if I could do this while I was a biology undergraduate at the National University of Singapore, I could achieve a lot more full-time. This was how I started Animal Concerns Research & Education Society (Acres) with nine other Singaporeans in 2001.

Over the last 14 years, we have successfully lobbied for harsher penalties for illegal wildlife traffickers, tipped off the Agri-Food & Veterinary Authority (AVA) to numerous offences committed by pet shops, traditional Chinese medicine shops and illegal collectors,

rescued more than 3,000 wild animals in Singapore and mobilised 20,000 volunteers. They man our 24-hour wildlife crime and rescue hotline, and, together with our 21 full-time staff members, represent us at roadshows, develop education programmes, help out at our bear sanctuary in Laos, and do our undercover work. We are lucky that those from Generation Y are keen on this issue.

Our goal is to start a movement, to get society involved in helping animals, and to expand into the region. It's not about building more shelters, but ending illegal wildlife trade so there is no need for the shelters. But we are nowhere near that now. What AVA needs to do is to increase its presence at our border checkpoints. There have been seizures in China or Vietnam of shipments which had stopped over in Singapore. When we do detect these illegal shipments, they are in the thousands – 1,000 star tortoises packed into a suitcase. And the next month, another 1,000. The frequency of these seizures shows you how many more shipments go undetected.

I've had setbacks. I have received death threats, had my front door splattered with red paint and the windows of my van smashed. In 2006, the contractor building our $650,000 shelter polluted the soil, and the shelter had to be demolished. Although the courts awarded us $26.5 million in damages, we have yet to receive a single cent from the contractor, who declared bankruptcy in 2012. We are making do with a smaller shelter built by our volunteers on undamaged land.

I keep going because animals are our moral responsibility. MP Seah Kian Peng said in 2007 that, for us to be in the top half of the First World, we must care for those who cannot speak and depend on us for the quality of their lives – animals. I take home a monthly salary of $2,500, and support my wife Amy, 38, who works part-time as group director of advocacy at Acres, and our one-year-old daughter. We live in an HDB flat in Jurong West and we don't have fancy dinners. But I go to work every day happy.

When Louis Ng was a volunteer keeper at the zoo in 1999, he spoke up against photography sessions with baby chimpanzees. His success with this led to him later working full-time to fight for animal rights.

My novel is about who we are

By day, architect Isa Kamari, 55, is in charge of ensuring that commuters have safe and pleasant journeys on public transport. By night, he writes stories and poems, and is the first part-time artist to have won the Cultural Medallion, in 2007

I published my first poem in 1979 and my first collection of short stories in 1993. But when friends urged me to write novels, I hadn't the courage or stamina.

But one day, my eldest daughter Dhuha, who was then eight, came home from school crying. I asked her why she was upset, and she said her Malay schoolfriends insisted she was Chinese, and so was an outsider among them.

My mother-in-law is Chinese, but had been adopted by a Malay family.

When I asked my wife Sukmawati how we should answer Dhuha, she handed me her draft PhD thesis. I read it and learnt of this concept called political culture which shapes a person's thoughts and feelings. That made me ponder what actually shaped a person – was it his race, skin colour or cultural background?

I talked to my mother-in-law about her life as a Chinese among Malays. I also read about the life of prominent Singaporean politician Yaacob Mohamed. All these influences came together in my first novel, *Satu Bumi* (One Earth), which took two years to write.

Satu Bumi is about a Chinese woman adopted by a Malay family who falls in love with a Malay politician. I tried to remove the emotional baggage with which our society is still burdened. We should start with the premise that everyone is different and that we've got to respect everyone's value systems, inclinations and preferences. Nobody should be seen as domineering; everybody has a voice.

I grew up in Kampung Tawakal, off Whitley Road, a village of many races within a Chinese cemetery. My father was a typewriter mechanic turned gardener and my mother a housewife. I topped my batch in primary school and got into Raffles Institution. I once won first prize in a national schools' poetry recital and one of the judges urged me to read poetry on national radio, which I did. That fuelled my interest in writing.

At university here, I learnt about Leonardo da Vinci and his idea of the multitalented Universal Man. That image stuck with me, as did Islam's notion of *insanul kamil* or the perfect man, one who is not only efficient in his daily living, but also appreciative of his inner life.

When my wife and two daughters are in bed, that's my time to write and I focus on that up till 3am. I take a nap and later, on the bus and train to work, continue creating my novels in my mind. I'm in my office by 7am.

In 2006, when I was told that a teacher here, Rosli Sidek, had nominated me for the Cultural Medallion, I thought: "If it comes, it comes. If not, thank you for nominating me." I was cautious then because veterans such as Suratman Markasan and Mohamed Latiff Mohamed, the man who had recommended me to national radio, had not yet won the Medallion then. I won the award but I refrained from entering my works for the Singapore Literature Prize from then on; I felt it would not be right if I were to keep winning.

I write in Malay so it is only practical that I publish all my works in Malaysia and Indonesia, whose readers are curious about what's happening to Malays here; there are few readers of serious Malay literature here.

My wife and writers Alfian Sa'at and Alvin Pang have translated many of my novels into English. *Satu Bumi* has been translated into Chinese and another novel, *Rawa*, will soon be in Chinese too. I am now negotiating with a Turkish publisher for *Menara* (The Tower), which is my meditation on progress Singapore-style.

Singapore is an economically advanced and technocratic place, but we need to balance such progress with the finer things in life – friendship, love and caring for one another. Otherwise, we'd be doing things without understanding why we're doing them, and alienate ourselves from life itself. I also believe that you must know who you are and where you belong, so the next step you take is grounded in your understanding of the past and your vision of the future.

Isa Kamari is the deputy director of commuter infrastructure at the Land Transport Authority. He is also the youngest Malay here to have won the Southeast Asia Write Award, the Cultural Medallion and the Tun Seri Lanang Award.

Leonard Tan became his own boss after leaving Yahoo!, making costly mistakes and learning along the way.

You must fail in order to succeed

Leonard Tan, 37, learnt from Yahoo! and is now chief executive officer of $10 million search engine marketing firm PurpleClick

When I first started playing the board game Monopoly with my elder son Justin when he was five years old, I would purposely make him lose so badly he'd become bankrupt. He used to get upset, but I did it to teach him to embrace failure – just because he lost today doesn't mean the next time, he's not going to win. This is a lesson I've learnt from running my own business, search engine marketing firm PurpleClick: You must fail in order to succeed.

When I started my business in 2006, my friends thought I was crazy. I had been working as a sales account manager for search engine Yahoo! for two years, earning about $10,000 a month, when I noticed a business opportunity. Clients from small and medium-sized enterprises were constantly asking me for free advice on online marketing on other search engines such as Google or MSN even though I worked for Yahoo!.

So with $100,000 in savings, I started PurpleClick in a rented space in a Chinatown shophouse. At the time, there were about 10 search engine marketing firms – helping businesses advertise on search engines – but nobody knew what PurpleClick was. Customers would think it was called Paper Clip or Purple Lick. Those who promised to follow me from Yahoo! backed out. Some even asked to check my identity card to make sure I wasn't scamming them.

Before PurpleClick, I ran two small businesses: an online one buying and selling university textbooks in the United States, where I did a master's degree in e-commerce at the Illinois Institute of Technology from 2002 to 2004, and a tuition business as a business student at the National University of Singapore from 1999 to 2002. It's easy to start a business, but not easy to scale it upwards.

From Yahoo! I learnt that systems and structures, such as fixed-format reports, structured meetings, forecasts and having projects in the pipeline, were very effective ways to help a company scale upwards. These were things I never thought about when running my previous businesses.

Using these lessons, I have grown PurpleClick into a $10 million business with almost 40 employees, an office here, one in Malaysia and one in the Philippines. In Singapore, we have moved into a new 4,600 sq ft office in Jalan Bukit Ho Swee.

We have long-term plans to expand within the region, but there is still a huge opportunity in the developed markets to increase online spending. So I encourage my staff to be entrepreneurial, to make decisions and changes where they see fit. I don't mind if they fail – there are some projects where we go in knowing we will fail – as long as they consider the possibility and consequences of failure.

I've had my share of failures. In PurpleClick's early years, I didn't automate our systems and processes quickly enough. This led to bottlenecks, disgruntled staff and unhappy customers. We eventually spent a six-figure sum to revamp our processes with technology.

Making mistakes is part of starting your own business. Too many young Singaporeans of my generation want a safety net before they are willing to take a risk, but I find that if an entrepreneur is not forced into a corner, the chances of him succeeding are low because he has nothing to lose. In Silicon Valley, it's the opposite.

The process to change mindsets about failure will take time, but I think this is the way we can have more global, iconic Singapore brands such as Osim, Creative, Charles & Keith and Sakae Sushi.

Science is not for the faint-hearted

Biologist Juliana Chan, 32, had a setback with her first doctorate project, but persevered with her nanoparticle research to score scientific breakthroughs

When I went to the Massachussetts Institute of Technology in 2006, I had never heard of nanoparticles. But here was this MIT professor, Robert Langer, speaking about nanoparticles. He said some people in his laboratory – which, with 150 people, is the world's biggest engineering lab – had made a chip with many pockets in it. These pockets contained drugs to treat disease, he said, and the chip was remote-controlled. So if you pressed remote control button A, pocket A would open to release drug A. And so on. This is an example of a medical device, which can be used to deliver drug doses into the body. So can nanoparticles, a thousand of which are the width of a strand of human hair.

After the talk, I went up to Prof Langer, who's a chemical engineer, and asked to join his lab. He said: "Go ahead, but I've never had a biology student." I said: "Give me a chance. I think this is cool."

As a scientist, you must find an idea cool to work on it. Otherwise, you can't be motivated because science is challenging. Everything you do is almost always failing; success is rare.

After I spent a year on my PhD project trying to make a nanoparticle to treat heart disease in Prof Langer's lab, one of my American colleagues came into the lab one afternoon and said: "Have you seen the latest issue of the *Proceedings of the National Academy of Sciences*?" I said: "No. Should I have?" And he said: "Maybe you should have a drink first."

Someone had published something similar to my project – before I had. All my studies and all the animals I had sacrificed for it! All for nothing. I was so depressed, I didn't work for a week. Later, my colleagues told me their own experiences of being beaten to publishing their findings. Science is not for the faint-hearted.

I grew up around East Coast Park and went to schools along Marine Parade Road. As an academic, I'm the odd one out in my family. My father Eric, a remisier, and mother Betty, an optometrist, never went to university. My sibling Samantha studied at a local university and is in marketing.

After topping my class at Katong Convent and completing my studies at Victoria Junior College, I wanted to study overseas. It happened that in 2003, the year I applied for an Agency for Science, Technology and Research (A*Star) scholarship, its chairman Philip Yeo had some grand plan for more women to do PhDs. It was just perfect timing; if I'd applied for it a year earlier, I would likely have gone on to a local university and taken on a desk job somewhere.

So I got into the School of Natural Sciences at Cambridge University, and after three years, went on to MIT for my PhD. My final PhD project, done with 10 colleagues, gave me three international patents. It involved putting sticky chains of amino acids shaped like hooks on nanoparticles and shooting these into the body via an IV drip. These sticky chains, which I call nanoburrs, are like the burrs on *lallang* (lovegrass). They bind to things they recognise as objects to which they need to bind, like one side of Velcro to another. For example, they stick like a Band-Aid to parts of artery walls damaged by balloon stents used to unblock arteries.

Nanoburrs can also deliver cancer-fighting drugs faster and more effectively to a patient, so he need not be infused with the drug for 12 hours at a go, three times a week.

I returned from MIT with my PhD – and my American husband Chester Drum, a cardiologist who now works here. We had worked together in Prof Langer's lab; being in the lab all day, it was the only way I'd meet someone. When Mr Yeo met Chester, he told me: "*Mai yi, song yi* (Buy one, get one free)."

Chester and I now have a daughter, Heather. I run my own lab at the Lee Kong Chian School of Medicine where I am an assistant professor and collaborate with Chester. We are trying to prevent heart attacks and strokes, as well as treat eczema more effectively.

Juliana Chan's work involves putting sticky chains of amino acids shaped like hooks on nanoparticles and sending these to specific areas in the body. The chains are like the burrs on *lallang* (lovegrass) and bind easily to targeted areas.

We celebrate Hari Raya, Christmas, Deepavali and Chinese New Year

Adam Maniam, a Tamil-Eurasian-Malay-Pakistani lawyer, is married to university sweetheart Yap Cuixian and they focus on shared values

Growing up, I thought it was the norm for everyone to celebrate both Hari Raya and Christmas, as we did in my family. Both occasions were equally important to us. We also celebrated Deepavali with our Hindu relatives and Chinese New Year with our uncles and aunts who married Chinese spouses.

It was only when I got to primary school that I realised from interacting with my friends that not everyone celebrated the same holidays and that my family was, in fact, a bit different.

My paternal grandfather was a Tamil Indian who was raised as a Hindu. He became a Roman Catholic when he married my Eurasian grandmother after World War II. Her father was a Tamil Indian, while her mother was Portuguese-Eurasian. They had nine children together, and raised them as Catholics.

My father attended Catholic schools for 12 years. His parents made sure they attended Sunday mass, and observed Christmas and Easter. But he, too, adopted a new faith when he married my mother in December 1977.

My mother is Muslim. Her mother is a Malay from Terengganu, while her father is Pakistani with a smattering of Chinese. My great-great-grandmother was a Chinese who was adopted as a baby by an Indian family in Singapore in the 1890s.

My parents fell in love after they met in 1973 as neighbours in Serangoon Gardens. They would hang out together with their siblings outside their homes, where they would spend leisurely evenings singing songs and playing the guitar. My mother said they didn't give the differences in their racial or religious backgrounds too much thought. It was only when marriage was discussed that she told him she could not marry a non-Muslim. He converted to Islam.

Dad says his family did not object to his change of religion, because both families had known each other well by then. There are also similarities between Catholicism and Islam, so it was not that big of an adjustment, he says. My younger brother Ashraf, 29, always playfully asks my father what pork tastes like, but he just smiles and says he doesn't remember, and that he never really liked pork anyway.

So my two brothers – one older, one younger – and I were raised as Muslims. We attended Islam classes. Still, on Christmas Eve, we would gather at my paternal grandmother's place with my cousins, and all of us would be peeping under the Christmas tree and guessing what our presents were. My mother would prepare classic Eurasian Christmas dishes such as curry devil – a very spicy curry flavoured with ginger, vinegar, mustard seed, onions and garlic – and chicken stew pie, and we would dig in as a family. We would also sing Christmas carols together. It was an open-minded upbringing and we were taught to accept people for who they were, rather than based on their race or religion.

This is why, when I married my university sweetheart Cuixian, who is ethnically Chinese and a free-thinker, we decided on a civil marriage. She strongly believes that every religion is correct and that you don't have to follow just one, and I respect her views. To be honest, my parents did have discussions with me about Cuixian being a non-Muslim before we got married. Her parents, too, were a little surprised at first when she told them she was dating an Indian Muslim, as her family is pretty homogenous. But over the six years we were dating, both families got to know us better and we are both fully integrated into each other's families now.

For us, doing good is more important than what you read or say, and we share these values despite our differences in culture and religion. After all, every religion, at its core, teaches you to do good. As for our one-year-old daughter Amelia, our plan is to teach her about what's out there and let her decide on her own.

In my view, the social interaction for most of Singapore has gone beyond mere tolerance. Race will matter less and less as we move forward because Singapore is becoming more multiracial. People are more exposed to different races and cultures, people will interact more with other races and cultures, and some blurring of lines and boundaries will be inevitable.

The Maniam family: (Standing on the left) Adam Maniam, 32, his wife Yap Cuixian, 30, with their daughter Amelia Ri-En, one. (Seated on the stairs) Elder brother Aaron, 36, and (bottom) younger brother Ashraf, 29. On the right are parents Sydney, 64, and Bibe Zoolaha, 59, and maternal great-grandmother Chan Bibi, 96.

My oxygen tank ran out on Everest

Jane Lee, 31, who co-founded and led the first women's expedition from Singapore to scale Mount Everest in 2009, talks about climbing the world's highest peak

Many people were sceptical when they heard that we were planning to climb Everest. People would come up to us at talks and be quite combative and rude. They would say things like: "I don't agree with what you're doing, it's very dangerous, it's very selfish. What about your parents?"

We were very affected at the start. Eventually, though, we just took it with a pinch of salt. All of us accepted that the endeavour itself was out of the ordinary – we were talking about women from Singapore mountaineering. It wasn't that the naysayers didn't believe in us, it was just that there was no precedent.

When we finally got to Everest, it was like, "Oh my God, at long last." At that point, we had been training for five years and putting our lives on hold for so long. But because we had trained so hard, Everest turned out to be something we had anticipated. It was a bit of that *kiasu* Singaporeanness – we really over-prepared.

There are environmental challenges, of course – bad weather, avalanches, ice blocks moving around. But the challenges go beyond that. The volume of oxygen that high up is also very low, and breathing alone becomes very stressful for your body. You don't sleep well because you are constantly in this hypoxic state. The expedition is also very long – three months of being cold, in a sleeping bag in a tent, not showering, not getting proper food – you're putting your body under stress on a day-to-day basis. You lose weight and you're susceptible to simple things like cough and cold that you never get over because your body doesn't have the immunity to recover.

I almost didn't make it to the summit. For the last part of the climb, we used supplementary oxygen. My oxygen system failed, and because there was all this wind blowing, I didn't hear the air leaking out of the tank. So when I got to the South Summit – which is about 1.5 hours from the true summit – I realised I was all out of oxygen. I stood there trying to fix the tank, and at one point got very light-headed. Fortunately, a Sherpa I had met at base camp came by with a client. I told him: "My oxygen is not working. Should I go up or come down? I'm lost." He just said: "Here, take mine", and gave me his bottle. He didn't need it because he was so fit. He really saved my summit attempt, because otherwise I would have had to go down, and I probably would have been in a very bad state from going down with no oxygen.

When I got to the summit, it was completely unbelievable. I just went: "Oh my God, I'm so lucky." We stayed there for only maybe 20 minutes, though. It wasn't like: "Oh yeah, let's celebrate!" It was more: "I'm here, let's take pictures, how much oxygen do I have? Let's go down." It was really, really cold, and we were still running on a finite amount of oxygen that we also needed for the descent.

When we made the summit, we were told that the server on our website almost crashed because we had so many well-wishers. And when we landed at Changi Airport and went to collect our bags at the baggage carousel, we suddenly heard this crazy screaming. All of us were thinking: "Were we on the same flight as some Taiwanese pop star?" Then we looked around, and saw it was for us. Friends, family and strangers were there to welcome us back.

When we first started, we didn't realise the extent of the impact it would have. When we see how the sport has grown here, when we see how many women are climbing, and not just climbing – there have been people who have come up to tell us that we inspired them to try something new – that has been very touching. Standing on the summit is a fleeting moment – in a way, you even forget about it – but what stays on is knowing you've inspired people to do something beyond what they thought was possible for themselves. To us, that's the true legacy of being in the team.

After her 2009 Everest climb, Jane Lee went on in 2011 to become the first woman from Southeast Asia to have scaled the highest mountains of each of the seven continents. Here she is seen at the top of the 6,168m Mt McKinley in Alaska, the highest peak in North America and one of the Seven Summits, in 2010.

Photo from JANE LEE

On Top of the World

For a small country, Singapore has produced a big number of world champs in many areas. Here's a crop of people who put the little red dot on the world map in their own chosen fields

Photo by BRYAN VAN DER BEEK

Vijayalakshmi Mohan, married mother of two and art therapist, 56

Guinness world record for creating the world's largest *rangoli* (a traditional Indian festive floor decoration made with coloured ground rice) measuring 2,756 sq ft on 3 August 2003 at Whampoa Community Club.

In India, where I was born, the belief was that the gods roamed the roads and so people would draw the biggest rangolis they could in front of their houses to attract the gods there. As a child, I used to think, I must draw the biggest rangoli on my road. I learnt how to draw from my mother, who would wake up at 5am daily to do so.

As it happens, I didn't draw the biggest rangoli on my road. But after migrating to Singapore in 1991 with my husband and children, I told myself: One day, I will draw the biggest rangoli in Singapore. In 2003, I completed my Guinness world record rangoli – on my own – in seven hours. I put the "Singapore's OK" logo in the middle because Singapore was just free of the Sars virus then.

I finished my feat at 2pm that day, and by 8pm, the cleaners had swept it all away! But that is the message of a rangoli – that nothing in life is permanent.

Sancy Suraj, founder and chief trainer of Pinnacle Minds, 30

Guinness world record for longest colour sequence memorised. Mr Suraj memorised a sequence of 160 randomly generated colours on a computer screen at the rate of 2 seconds per colour. He then proceeded to write the entire sequence on a piece of paper with a perfect score. This feat was achieved at ITE College East on 14 April 2012.

I definitely felt proud to not only get that record for myself, but also for my country.

Gamer Ho Kun Xian, 25

World champion Street Fighter 4 at Evolution 2013 in Las Vegas. Mr Ho, who has been gaming since he was seven, was the first Singaporean to win at this tournament, the world's largest fighting game competition.

I think it was really exciting to be standing on a stage in front of 6,000 people. No Singaporean had made it up there before. Winning the whole championship was something I never expected. It was definitely the most amazing lifetime experience that one could ever have.

Singaporean band
MONSTER CAT
made up of members
Psycho Cat, Hentai
Cat and Merta Cat

The band's single, *Tower*, from the album *The Violet Hour* was crowned Single of the Week on the global iTunes store in March last year, a first for a Singaporean band.

The build-up to the launch of our new album was a whirlwind combination of uncontrollable excitement and exhausting hard work – we had poured our hearts and souls into making this record and it was now down to the final leg of crazy logistics, admin and coordination work to get it out to people. In a way, it was like planning your own birthday party, before you are born.
*   When Tower was named iTunes Single of the Week, it was like the party now had huge rainbow streamers, dancing clowns on unicycles, a giant cake with fairies on it and a playpen with ponies. We were told it was the first time for a Singapore act to have their track chosen to be Single of the Week. It was thrilling and very flattering.*

Poet Desmond Kon, 45

Winner of the Poetry World Cup in 2014. Literary journal *The Missing Slate* picked poems by poets from 32 different countries that had been published in its journal the previous year. Readers voted for the winners via an online poll. In the finals, Singapore won with 1,295 votes to Pakistan's 1,270.

My poem, called "gǎn qíng yòng shì :: impulsive and impetuous", is one vignette of a much longer sequence of prose poems that revolve around the life of Gigi. When I was checking the score for the final, it was neck and neck. The last two hours were terrifying to watch. I hadn't eaten the whole day. My first meal was at 6pm that day.
*   People were just unbelievably supportive – votes came in from abroad as well, from Australia, Indonesia, Korea, the Philippines, the UK and the US. Because the final is completely reliant on readers' votes, this is a country win, and it couldn't have happened without everyone's amazing energy and spunk.*

We're now so much more...

Singapore has achieved much but are its people of First World standard?
Well, more or less, according to *Straits Times* cartoonist Adam Lee

2005 — 2014

2005

- From 1 January, civil servants start a **five-day work week**

- On 22 July, the **National Library Board**'s $203 million new headquarters opens in Victoria Street, replacing its old home in Stamford Road (seen here), which closed in 2004

- Swimmer **Joscelin Yeo** wins six gold medals at the SEA Games in Manila, making a career haul of 40, the most of any athlete in the Games' history

2006

- In his Budget speech on 17 February, Prime Minister Lee Hsien Loong announces a **$2.6 billion progress package**, the biggest in Singapore history; it includes generous CPF top-ups, work bonuses and rewards for National Servicemen

- On 16 March, Toa Payoh resident Thomas Pung serves Britain's **Queen Elizabeth II** a drink with the same glass that she drank from when she first visited his family's flat in 1972

- On 7 December, President SR Nathan opens the **National Museum** after a $132.6 million refurbishment over 3½ years

2007

- From 1 February, most low-income Singaporean workers will get cash incentives to stay employed with the **Workfare Income Supplement Scheme**

- On 30 June, the **National Stadium** closes after 34 years of the Kallang Roar

- Singapore Airlines is the first carrier in the world to fly the world's largest aircraft, the **A380-800**, with a maiden flight between Singapore and Sydney on 25 October

- Crooner **Hady Mirza**, the second Singapore Idol, beats five regional rivals to win the first Asian Idol competition on 17 December in Indonesia

2008

- On 8 February, **Ah Meng**, the zoo's beloved orang utan, dies of old age. Four thousand people attend her burial

- On 27 February, **Mas Selamat Kasturi**, leader of terrorist group Jemaah Islamiyah, escapes from detention here; he is recaptured in April 2009 in Malaysia

- In August, women paddlers Wang Yuegu, Feng Tianwei and Li Jiawei give Singapore its **second Olympic silver medal**

- On 28 September, Fernando Alonso wins the world's **first Formula 1 night race** here

2009

- In May, Prime Minister Lee Hsien Loong sets up the **Economic Strategies Committee** to study ways to restructure the economy, including measures to boost productivity

- On 16 May, about 1,000 people in various shades of pink turn up at Speakers' Corner for the first **Pink Dot** meet to support those with alternative lifestyles

- On 6 November, China agrees to **lend Singapore two pandas** for 10 years; on 6 September 2012, pandas Kai Kai (above) and Jia Jia arrive here from Chengdu

- On 27 December, Singapore's **biggest bus interchange** costing $24 million opens at Boon Lay

Singaporeans want a bigger say in shaping the nation's future, which includes enhancing the sense of being Singaporean

2010

- From 12 January, parents of different races can now **double-barrel** their children's race – Chinese-Indian for example – on their children's birth certificates and identity cards

- On 14 February, the first of Singapore's **two integrated resorts**, Resorts World at Sentosa, opens for business; on 27 April, Marina Bay Sands (above) follows suit

- On 24 May, Singapore and Malaysia agree to **move the railway station** from Tanjong Pagar to Woodlands, resolving a 20-year tussle over railway land

- **Flash floods** occur in June and July, affecting parts of Orchard Road for the first time in 25 years

- In August, Singapore hosts the inaugural **Youth Olympic Games**, drawing 3,600 youths from 205 nations here

2011

- In a **watershed general election** on 7 May, the Workers' Party takes Aljunied-Hougang GRC, leading George Yeo and Lim Hwee Hua to resign as ministers. Minister Mentor Lee Kuan Yew retires from the Cabinet

- Singaporeans elect **Dr Tony Tan Keng Yam** as their seventh president after a four-cornered fight

- On 8 October, the entire $10 billion **Circle Line** is up and running, marking operator SMRT's 24th anniversary

- Between 14 and 17 December, **MRT services are disrupted**, triggering a slew of repairs

2012

- Singapore returns to the Malaysia Cup and the Malaysia Super League this year with a young squad known as **LionsXII**; in 2013, the team tops the Malaysia Super League

- The south end of Singapore's largest public park, **Gardens by the Bay**, the size of 177 football fields, opens on 29 June

- In August, Singapore's women paddlers win another two **Olympic medals** in London

- On 13 October, the first **Our Singapore Conversation** is held to give Singaporeans a say in how their future should be shaped

2013

- In January, the government releases a **Population White Paper** that projects a population of 6.9 million here by 2030; this leads to protests against having more foreigners here

- From 24 June this year till 23 June 2015, commuters **travel for free on the MRT** if they exit any one of 16 downtown stations before 7.45am

- At noon on 21 June, the haze worsens the air quality here, with the **Pollutant Standards Index hitting a record of 401**

- On 8 December, mobs turn violent and **riot in Little India**, attacking emergency vehicles after an Indian national is crushed by a bus there; 25 people are charged

- Film-maker Anthony Chen's movie *Ilo Ilo* becomes **Singapore's most awarded film internationally**. Its wins include four major Golden Horse awards and the Cannes Camera d'Or

2014

- On 9 February, Prime Minister Lee Hsien Loong announces the $8 billion **Pioneer Generation Package**, focused on health care, for about 450,000 elderly people aged 65 or older this year and who became Singaporeans before 1987

- The world's largest dome, spanning 12 Olympic-sized swimming pools, is unveiled on 28 June when the new 55,000-seater **National Stadium** opens here

- Between July and August, Singapore and Malaysia both increase the **charges for foreign-registered vehicles** to enter one another's countries

- On 2 September, the massive **Jurong Rock Caverns** open; they are Southeast Asia's first underground store for liquid hydrocarbons

This is Home, Truly

Singaporeans are rooted to home because of places they love and which they hold fond memories of

The zoo is one of my favourite places. I've been there two times, once with my teacher and class, and the second time with my family and some friends. I like to see the animal show where the elephant sprays water, and I love the horse ride. My favourite animal is the white tiger because it has stripes on its body and it can swim very well. In this photo I'm with my younger sister Adreana and two friends.

Aleesya Isham, nine (second from left), Primary 3, Pioneer Primary School

My office overlooks Marina Bay. I like how so much happens on these waters: celebrations, memories, wishes, regattas, light shows. It is a reflection of our progress but it should also become a reflection of our values. Everyone needs a mirror; this is Singapore's mirror.

Amerson Lin, 32, who works in business development

Our love for nature brought my wife and me to Pulau Ubin, and we often went there on dates. We decided to have our pre-wedding shoot there as well because it looked like another Singapore altogether – away from urban living.

Photographer Zakaria Zainal, 30, with his wife Aqilah Zailan, 26

To me, Little India is quintessential Singapore. It's a heady mix of colour, spices, perfume and incense. A seamless blend of tradition and modernity, where you find objects that would seem to be at home in a maharaja's palace being hawked next to the latest mobile phone. It's a clash of the incessant honking of cars, buses, taxicabs, with the peace of the inner belly of a temple. To some, it's chaos. To me, it's bliss.

Teacher Ann Cheo, 34

Around 15 years ago, I became interested in plants, so I bought and memorised a book of the biological names and descriptions of 300 plants and trees. Then I joined a volunteer group to learn how to guide visitors around the Botanic Gardens. It's an amazing place and I always enjoy explaining the wonders of the rainforest to visitors. Knowing plants and trees by their names makes them your friends. I wish more people would make time to visit the Botanic Gardens. There's so much to learn there.

Ameerali Abdeali, 64, retired civil servant

My family chose to live at the fringe of the Lower Seletar Reservoir because we love nature. We get to enjoy the crisp fresh air every morning, the sounds of birds and crickets, and the abundance of wildlife, even in our garden. We love to stroll along the water's edge and at times even try our luck at fishing. We were delighted when the area was developed into the Springleaf Nature Park which instantly became a playground for my grandchildren. This is also an outdoor classroom for them, as I can impart my knowledge of flora and fauna to them. Where else, other than Singapore, can one live in a city and have nature at the doorstep?

Butterfly guidebook author Steven Neo, 65, with grandchildren Trent, one year old, and twins Natalie (left) and Naomi, five

We love the National Stadium because it's beautiful and special, both inside and out. I used to go to the old National Stadium all the time, ever since I was a boy, to watch football in the old days of the Malaysia Cup. I'm a big football fan and I remember that I always wanted to play a game in that old stadium, but I never got a chance to. My Dad used to take me there, and now I take my son and daughter to the new stadium. Besides the football matches, we also love to shop and dine in the mall. Our kids also enjoy romping in the playground.

Music teacher Chris Lesslar, 42, seen here with his wife Monica and their children Camille, eight, and Craigston, five

We love spending time at Bishan Park. It truly is a one-stop shop for our family. It has ample activities for my toddler, my husband is here every weekend playing soccer, and it helps me keep fit by enticing me to go on jogs on weekday mornings.

Bhavani Melvin, 32, stay-at-home mother, with husband Melvin Arulanthu, 36, and son Nicholas, two

The wide, green space of Marina Barrage and how it overlooks the gorgeous Singapore cityscape attract us. Many families go there, especially on weekends, to relax and fly a kite or two, so there's a great family atmosphere. We're hoping to start a little family tradition of our own by taking our son there more regularly to fly kites.

Lecturer Leong Wee Keat, 34, who goes to the Barrage with his son Matthew, two, and wife Carolyn Quek, 31, a teacher

I love Newton Hawker Centre more out of nostalgia than anything. I used to come here a lot with my family when I was young and one of my favourite memories is that of one National Day, when after watching the parade live, my family drove through the jam from the National Stadium to eat chicken wings here. I still remember how hungry I was and how I grabbed the wings so fast that they burnt my fingers. To this day, barbecued chicken wings are my favourite thing to eat here.

Teacher Shuli Sudderuddin, 31

Age: 13
Md Hasbi

Age: 12
Jun Hao

Age: 12
Lim Ching Lih

Age: 11
Yeong Zhi Wen

Body expression is one of the important ways of communication used by the students at the Singapore School for the Deaf. This photo taken in 1999 shows the students in a classroom at the school, established in 1963.

Photo by ALAN LIM

Bird lovers gather every Sunday at the void deck of an HDB block at Ang Mo Kio Street 41 to admire the birds and listen to them sing, as seen in this photo taken in 2014.

Photo by HANG LOO MING

Children running about an inflatable installation in the shape of the iconic 1970s dragon playground slide on the front lawn of the National Museum. The play area was part of the museum's Masak Masak: My Childhood exhibition in May 2014, a programme in the seventh annual Children's Season line-up.

Photo by KEVIN LIM

S League chief executive Lim Chin (centre) and players of various football teams showing off their body paint at the S League fanfare event at Orchard Road in February 2013. The event was used to kickstart the mission to get fans into stadiums across the island to support the new season of the S League, which was launched in 1996.

Photo by GAVIN FOO

Children and their fathers running at the 800m Father and Child Challenge Race during the 23rd edition of the Safra Singapore Bay Run and Army Half Marathon, flagged off from Esplanade Bridge, on 31 August 2014.

Photo by KEVIN LIM

Index

Acknowledgements

For the Esplanade photo on pages
130-131, we would like to thank

- Esplanade – Theatres on the Bay
- Makeup Entourage
- Make Up For Ever
- Redken
- Rasel Catering
- Second Charm

For the National Stadium photo on
pages 154-155, we would like to thank

- Sport Singapore
- Singapore Sports Hub

We would like to thank Glenn Phua for letting
us reproduce his drawings on the inside front
and back covers of the book

We would also like to thank photographer
Hang Loo Ming for allowing us to use his photo
on pages 188-189

And special thanks to the following from
Singapore Press Holdings:

Editorial Projects Unit,
English/Malay/Tamil Media Group

The Straits Times Picture Desk

Information Resource Centre, in particular
Sim Peng Kwang and Kong Yoke Mun